About the Author

I was born during dark communism in Prague, Czechoslovakia.

My future life and prospects were determined forever by the forced decision imposed upon my father and his brother.

Both had fought Hitler's Fascism in the Czech Free Army, under British Command. They had survived six years as proud patriots, fighting for their homeland in various countries, and for freedom, everywhere.

They returned to their Prague intending to start life anew. With the handover of the country to Stalin and his repressive Communism, they both, with impassioned reluctance, sought to emigrate, together with their respective families, to leave behind yet another imposed totalitarianism.

The regime permitted only one family to leave, with just one suitcase.

Faced by this devastating reality, my father and his brother could find only one solution.

They tossed a fateful coin!

Two families were forever torn asunder.

One family visa was granted, for Australia.

From that very moment, my life and future, and that of my parents, was forever based on that toss of that coin.

My parents and I sailed to Melbourne as refugees.

My aunt, uncle and cousins remained for the next forty years, living under Communist tyranny.

I learnt English, finished my schooling, then four years of Visual Art studies, and with fearless optimism, started my first truly individual steps into my own life.

As a professional artist, I have a life endlessly enriched by extraordinary people, episodes, serendipity, and creativity, in many countries, living across borders of the world, exhibiting, with my works represented in many National, State, and Regional collections.

At the time of publishing, I am based in Prague.

** I have left an interesting quandary for the reader to discover, in *FIFTY POEMS BY T. E. FANTL*. Perhaps deliberately. Perhaps by chance.

Clue: Perhaps T. E. FANTL is 'additionally' challenged?!

Fifty Poems

T. E. Fantl

Fifty Poems

Olympia Publishers
London

www.olympiapublishers.com
OLYMPIA PAPERBACK EDITION

Copyright © T. E. Fantl 2024

The right of T. E. Fantl to be identified as author of
this work has been asserted in accordance with sections 77 and 78
of the Copyright, Designs and Patents Act 1988.

All Rights Reserved

No reproduction, copy or transmission of this publication
may be made without written permission.
No paragraph of this publication may be reproduced,
copied or transmitted save with the written permission of the
publisher, or in accordance with the provisions
of the Copyright Act 1956 (as amended).

Any person who commits any unauthorised act in relation to
this publication may be liable to criminal
prosecution and civil claims for damage.

A CIP catalogue record for this title is
available from the British Library.

ISBN: 978-1-78830-962-2

This is a work of fiction.
Names, characters, places and incidents originate from the writer's
imagination. Any resemblance to actual persons, living or dead, is
purely coincidental.

First Published in 2024

Olympia Publishers
Tallis House
2 Tallis Street
London
EC4Y 0AB

Printed in Great Britain

Acknowledgements

One day in London at a favorite pub, the "Queens" in Tryon Street, Chelsea, Maggie Mee, my partner, and I, were sitting at an outside table.
Beautiful weather.

I was writing in a notebook.

I always carry a sketchbook, as well as a notebook.

By profession I am an established practicing and exhibiting Visual Artist.

Maggie, seeing that I was writing, asked what I was doing. I replied that I was writing poetry.
 I was now exposed, akin to that very first solo exhibition, decades ago, when, for the first time, my paintings and drawings were hung on gallery walls.
 Maggie asked me could she read some of my works.

The fact of the matter is that I have been writing poetry since my late teens. Very, very privately.
 Since childhood, I have always loved language and its sheer potent and descriptive endless possibilities.
 Over the decades, I have written a vast amount of poetry, but always, and only, for me.
 No one had ever been told.
 I have, so far, filled three volumes, manuscripts, into

which I have crafted my words, thoughts, interplays of experiences and observations, with tossed in imagination.

Maggie finished reading several works and asked me pertinent questions.

Without telling me, she audaciously sent six poems to Olympia Publishers for consideration.

Their response was a request for 50 poems to be published as a book — this book.

After selecting the poems, these handwritten works, in very small writing, had to be typed and edited.

Maggie sat, for more than nine months, scrutinising each word, line, and punctuation, as she typed.

I am profoundly grateful to Maggie, firstly for that audacious belief in my poems, and for her meticulous and patient assistance to me, often with insightful wisdom, to prepare all the fifty works for production.

My gratitude to Maggie is all-the-more profound, as had she not 'discovered' my poetry, there would, more likely than not, never have been a published book of any of my written works.

T. E. FANTL

Front Cover – Section from the painting
"The Real Full Story - Episode 3" 2019 by Tomas Fantl.
Back Cover - "Shadow Self Portrait" photograph by Tomas Fantl

Contents

SNIPPETS FOR REAL!! 11
SLIGHT 18
TRISTAN'S TRYSTS! ...,....... 25
INSIDE THE HOLY TOASTER 30
RESPITE 33
CRITICS (WITH SOME RHYME) 34
SMOKE RINGS 38
SPREAD OUT 41
PERSONAL PERSON 42
THE GREEK 43
BLIND DATES 46
SUNDAYS 47
PRINCE OF BOHEMIA 52
SMUDGE 63
THE PAINTER — THE DECADE 67
PENNY ARCADE 70
JSEM ČECH! ... CZECH I AM! 71
SOMETHING 77
A MIX OF REALITY 79
DON'T 86
THE AMERICAN 88
PASSION-PORTFOLIO 91
THE EXHIBITION 93
COFFEE SHOPPE 97
WHAT I'VE DONE ... I'VE DONE IT! 98

HA! HA! HA! HA! HA!	101
THE PIMP	105
HIERATH	108
THE RHUBARBARIAN	111
GHOSTY	117
ODE TO MYSELF	121
WHACKY THURSDAY	126
HEART!	132
PULL ON YOUR TIGHTS!	136
ABSURD WITH TABASCO SAUCE	138
LIDO DI CLASSE	141
AGO	143
THE SAGE	145
ENTRE CÔTE	148
BABBLE	149
ON	152
TRAPEZE	154
BENDED FLESH	157
DEJEUNER SUR L'HERBE … LUNCHEON ON THE GRASS	167
CALLITHUMPIANS	168
SHORT SYNOPSIS	170
WINTER'S ONSET	172
JUST "ABOUT"	179
CONSEQUENT INCONSEQUENCE	181
SUCH IT IS	184

SNIPPETS FOR REAL!!

Well!! Did you ever
spit on the flight?
Well, did you ever
grin on the hop?
Who am I to know
when writing this?
I skim my thoughts
I slash the paint
He empties his glass
poured down the throat

The barman couldn't care their swill
mops his surface, meets no eyes.
"Give me another!"
- he cares for nought.
The Union Jack hovers
above all reach.
Oscar Wilde's ghost vacates
as Spitfire beer aligns with others.
Patrons claim their seats
conjuring glasses and crisps.

Goya hangs luminous in etchings dark.
Realities in mirrors leave no consequence.
He talks to her, she politely responds
awaiting her moment's leave.
Old is all new, just waiting time
serious issues feign relevance
but no one cares of other's stuff
looking for exit to flee and leave.
The two young women talk of their beaus
gossip searching age old answers.

The naked painter melts in the rain
fused, spattered oil paint holds him together.
He enters the 'Queens' crimsoned in heat
finds a corner and sits, sluicing his teeth with his tongue.
"Today everything is so expensive!"
old dear says to her pal
at precisely the same second as millions say same
across the world, at same time.
They both wear black and white tops,
striped across in couched widths
their accents estranged, hushed tones unite,
fish 'n' chips eaten to plate.

Well!! Did you ever
swill endless pints
or savour the dram of vodka's warmth,
swelling confidence!
Close can be love, closer be self,
the slurry of life slides off the oil.
Two aged actresses gossip their fill
in English accents so toff.
First says "I had Dicky, but it wasn't to be.
Knee-jerk, on contact, so, so divine.
Utterly enchanting, he was a gem you know.
Oooh, so totally, totally self-absorbed!"

Second chirps "I took George Bundy to bed with me.
His was tiny - I never saw it, so surprised was I
Yuh! You can't compete with other women.
He gave up drinking, died two weeks later
Last time I saw him he was sitting under a table
already expelled, already bad news."
She grizzles in hoary bel canto cadence
bleeding her positioned reminisce.

Back to the first, she careens on and on
"She was the mistress of the grandmother!!
She was born Greszevsky you know.
The brother was Vladimir. He was nifty!
She got into the bath, too weak to get out,
she was likely to have heart-flushes!
Ah! Ha!! She was the painter, Mary Cassatt you know.
You know that kind of thing?
Then there was Churchill's alcoholic daughter, the redhead.
I met her at the farm.
Now please, if you will, I was not interested
I thought, just go, just go!!
If a guy is really old, one must work the opposite way,
when push comes to shove, do the shopping!!"

The other chips in, "I could have had thirty to dinner.
Ticky and Bicky gave interesting conversation
a most enchanting conversation.
I pointed out to my new best friend so sweet,
and her pappa would have been hot and cold,
in Delhi at a government hotel you know.
I must have been twenty, and then he said
there was somebody he knew in Geneva.
Call me up, and I'll do it.
Just send a cable and sign my name.
So I went over, checked in at the Imperial
he just came up, he wasn't a great poet
but summed up the situation of the times.
I've been coming back indefinitely, not being a bore!"

They both up and left, deciding payment by card
their afternoon spent, next week to return.
The painter, I sit, so English this hour
the toffs are gone, the theatre is spent.
Extraordinary, extraordinary, the swathes of this town
the half-moon melds with grand Union Jack.
The Indian Summer November bound
back to my poetry, whatever that is.
Now the Germans garnish their chairs
outside the 'Queen's Head', the dog pulls on leash.
I still can't believe you, London Town
no matter the derision those back there throw me.

Next table to me, he's been back to Bruges
on the ferry for nineteen pounds there and back.
Squints at his sitter, polishes his lens
ink runs dry in my pen.
Says "'E's a geezer! Bloody 'ell", he quips
"a tosser, a lag 'e once was.
A schemer, a planner, not the full quid.
'e owes me, 'ere, get me some chips".
The artist swivels on bottom's hard seat
now jotting free-wheeling prose.
Heat teams with cold, human heat on the up
windows cascading the wet.

Well! Did you ever
watch through the room
where rent boys do what for their purse
and slave eye to eye the luck of their draw,
to spill of their seconds
to fleece of their moments.
A door frees and opens
as velvet cleaves shut
as ghostly shadows vacate.
So much pervades the seconds on seconds
enter and exit, disappear!

The young duet sits, he to she
small talk competes for game's end.
She sits oozing sex, he sits, all erect
wanting to reach life's climax.
Seagulls call, as British seagulls do
A studio is what he desires
to paint on large scale
enough of A4 to paint cadence in suites.
He moves to apartment bit by bit over days
to leave Limegrove's basement of months.
The real start of real life, the wait now at end
tethered to nothing, London to claim.

Well!! Did you ever
take chance, slave to nought
did you even downsize to live
perpetuity of days left, deflect their denials.
Ignore who negate, shrug off all their bleats
disregard the others, ignore expectations
spit on all who deign failure
deny them, complete.
Doomsayers are tossed
I thrill in whatever
sometimes the ups, less sometimes the downs
I live complete through it all, so complete.

Well! I'll do ever
but more do I do.
Sequestered to my life
it's nobody's business
the painter, perhaps poet
will live his full fill.
Go burn your trees and go burn one life
I've burnt my burns
another day's gleams fill.
Let me paint on, write in my manner
behoved to no-one but me.

28 – 31 October 2014
London, England

SLIGHT

Slight curled lip
Slight cold smile.
Slight the mendacious
excuses unfurled.
Slight as she sits
so lost in her chair.
Slight mister bow-tie
coming in here.

"Pisses me off, luv"
he throws to her space.
"I left India for all this!"
he seeks to command.
Slight is her look
then looks far away,
as he gasps at her silence —
no engagement is made.

Dust off the fallow fields
awaiting full life.
Dust off the habitude
shafting its gift!
Pleas for more time
enter no gods ears
The crow pecks slight moments

never knowing an end.
Slight cold lip
Slight cold smile
sits frozen in nothing
awaiting no promise.
Lost in her chair
sips on glass of cold wine
spilling her moments,
running out are birth's seconds.

Slight is the wine
it doesn't do much.
Slight is her pulse
never speeding on chance.
Slight is the trumpet
heralding tempts.
Slight is the grave
sealing the end.

She sits as many wait,
day in and day out
ensconced in that wait
ensconced in time lost.
Slight is the curled lip
as slight is the smile.
The crow pecks all up
fulfilled in its pecks.

She remembers not much
as not much has evented.
She remembers no touch
as touch made no dent.
Slight is shallow memory
Slight memory of each 'him'
Slight is her memory
of nothing to claim.

Slight her curled lip
Slight cold is her smile.
She is all others
as others are she.
Cleaved to their wait
but wait has no merit.
The crow has no wait
takes advantage of all!

He still looks full on
charting no course.
Running the moments
knowing parlance.
Yet splurging no words
craves sweet some moments.
He curls tightened lip
hedonistic, but bluff.

Her image cajoles
to meet in the mirror.
Repeating reflection
from what there sits.
Like a connecting flight
she melts the glass.
Meeting herself
through the other side.

She strains lower arms
her hands pushing up.
The thin heavy on bone
straining for comfort.
She strains to remember,
but not then much.
One Christmas night falters,
and then it's out,
long before Christmas performs.

Wanting some comfort
wanting some sex.
Wanting some touch
wanting caress.
Wanting warm kiss
wanting empty promise.
The crow rips the guts
from a morsel, once life.

At narrow blind corner,
white as his collar
the young new-bred priest
pulses fast by.
Anchored to bicycle
cassock all airborne
filling the street
confessing to all.

She hears nothing of hope
for hope sits in nothing.
Nothing gives nothing
her glass gives her hope!
Her glass filled to top
then gulped to the mid
then drunk to the empty
glass filled with hope - gone!

He offers her another
she accepts with a nod.
Her lids on the droop
no interest for his.
Sluices it down
her head on the bob.
Bag on her arm
another night done.

Slight sagged her lip
gone is cold smile.
Gone is her 'posh'
in many years long past.
Pushes on chair
the pub is a-spinning.
Now cares for nothing,
her nothing is now!

He paces towards her
three paces, and back.
Watching her spinning,
her world complete skew!
No, not her world!
Her life in the glass.
The crow sits await,
to tear at her fall.

She gets up to stagger
perhaps stagger to fall.
Bled from her cross
her burden of life.
None cares her consequence
as none cares her lot.
The crow cares for all of her
bespoke lustrous feathers to fill.

She had curled lip
She had cold smile
She was slightly mendacious
gave excuses unfurled.
She had miniscule moments
unfurled on life's hill.
The crow waited, devoted
to her body and soul.

9 – 13 December 2014
London, England

TRISTAN'S TRYSTS!

It's a sundial morning.
The shadows are in!
Rousseau's tiger fends the grass.
As pentimento, in layers of green.

The bed creaks!
The humid mummified mattress is stained
as the Turin Shroud!
Somewhere deep within
a coil "thwank!!!s" — suddenly —
as if the last heartbeat.

Louche Tristan sidles from the bed.
Twists out the door, slides on cobbles, wet.
Curses through worn teeth, wrinkled at eye,
the blazing blue burns, as his fire and rage.
A few steps on, the Prague pub is hot.
Bohemian songs swill as black is the beer.

Same beggar, prostrate, all dignity spent.
His head far below each passer-by's step!
There are no kings, no princesses more.
Yet everywhere still they all hold court!
Citizens clinch them, above all invasions.
Kafka still metamorphosing; Svejk still chortles.

Pallid Tristan, animus of life!
Lopes as Prague's Golem, inert in his head.
Indigo cumulus fills to full.
Then explodes with Thor's crack!!,
brutally ricocheting from all Prague's gold.
The beautiful storm cascades!

Humidity sags to cobbled streets
slipping from steep red tiled roofs.
Tristan swells, his sweat awash
cursing hot drips from his pits!
Cool jazz soothes my temples, smartens me sharp
joining my pictures and words.

Charcoal smoulders, indigo to black!
Microphone, illicit, soft to loud!
His eye squints from haze to focus!
Dormant comes alive and squirms in disarray!
Music squeals its blunt crescendo!
Brown beer, black beer, Tristan swills his fill!

He wanders aloof, heel on the thud,
hunched over his racing shadow.
Calcified teeth, glued stupefied grin,
squealing his ambiguous thoughts!!
Tristan trounces all in his path
Lascivious mission his bent!

Thor repeats his clamorous clout
drenching his supine hoards.
Laggards, lords, disciples, queens!
Numerics rumble alchemists' brains
Trams rumble cobblestoned rails!
Not-much squeaks in Tristan's brain — opiate!

Tristan's trysts in gnarled intent,
not considered, made on his run.
The Jews, the Christians, the malcontents
sweep his path, coddle his fillip.
She swirls her petticoats, dress atop
Tousled blond hair slaving bare shoulders.

Shunned by the sundry, if not by all
Riffs echo on hills!
He steers his path, oblivious of its course
as a blinkered horse, blinded.
Meter by meter his trajectory shortens
but with no end-point, commits.

Her perfumed drops dovetail her wake
Heads rotate at her smell and sight.
Taut barking beasts regale from her scent
Seconds tighten with every step!
Expectations shudder, blood warmth bleached.
A crowd forms, distilled of breath!

Tristan pouts, then lower lip flops!
Eyes glaze, he twists on leathered heels.
Staccato!! The pause! The violent sniff!
Splayed leathered toes, bulbous as paws!
A fly lands to taste the ooze from his snout,
then terminates with fetid disgust!

She squanders no moment, no neurosis like his!
— and dwells on the apotheosis of her time.
Flowers on the balcony bow in the breeze
The crescendo of imminence massages the crowd.
Here-to and where-not slaves the narrow path.
Blue-grey and white cobbles tilt each made step.

He lurches, she glides, the duel skives their steps.
Pauses, his head turns, ear to the wind.
Downwind scant, her perfume, breaches his nostrils
Then tosses violent snarl of fetid disgust.
Narrow the stoned path skews at the corner
His crazed head rolls, hers claimed high.

Tight are his fists craving to punch
His battle descends a bit and a quarter.
The wafts of two smells fracture soft breeze
Sooth is the sayer crashing the wind!
Both transmit their blaze of glory —
Like limpets glued they cleave the path.

Prague's descant screams!
Steepled gargoyles vibrate!
Did I hear my phone ring
to distract me from this?
Some canine barks at his malodourous breath!
She's upbeat!

One minus one — no space left.
Tristan stomps — the ant lies crushed.
She sees a Golem mindless — red hot.
He fends! She twists!
Inane cur slumps his clay
and capricious spiders gather.

His sticky mass heaves on the ground.
His languid groans pervades each one.
His slime of chance drools white cascades,
his time embalmed in muck.
Crowd murmurs.
Child strains.

She sees nothing!
The duel is won!
Instant! Elegant! Untempted!
Won!
Dismissed!
She glides!

1 July – 3 August 2016 Prague, Czech Republic

INSIDE THE HOLY TOASTER

Tall!
Abundant Leaf!
Verdant!
Yet the light slips through
spaces.
The spaces of breath.
Past the balcony!
Past glasses of Merlot!
Past staccato conversation.
Past slender eye contact.

They had a maid.
In Knightsbridge!
Forty-five years ago.
There's a plot in the cemetery,
the third row in.
She died in sixty-one.
Bedridden she was.
They don't let weeds grow.
Weedless!
It looks bloody horrible

The grave has sunk.
You can see down the gap.
It all becomes important!
Or does it?
He died of appendicitis
in forty-two.
Not making no bones about it now.
Yet moss, the moss, glowing verdant.
Lush, wee renewal
as primeval forest.

But, aglow!
All night the tower burned.
From four to twenty-four ablaze!
The smoking vivid torch
now a pyre of human ages.
Upward the lift,
cascading the tumult.
The rich turn the cheek,
sip cooling wine.
Not their problem!
Leave it to politics!
Deleted!

Hark the herald angels … ?
Don't stop the trapeze girl
on her swing!
Snap the book shut!
Pay the toll!
Espy the waitress
spin on her heel!
Pop the cork on another round.
The falcon dives,
the pigeon falls.

Proud was the maid who cleaves the dust.
Forthright was the proud festering man.
Dogs sniff dogs' arses to determine friend.
Janitors work if not for filth.
Coins of reward occasion on streets.
Argued philosophies tighten rabid borders.
But she and he sleep in their bones.
Their crescendo of calm —
Replete!!

4 – 7 July 2018
Prague, Czech Republic

RESPITE

The respite.
The time between stop and start.
Between breathe out and in.
Between stare and blink.
Between listen and hear.
Between sound and silence.
Between second and hour.
Between peace and battle.
Between sad and smile —
and then the laugh.
Between stand-off and love.
Between work and rest.
Between wake and sleep.
Between hot and cold.
Between duet and solo.
Between hurry and tarry.
Between take and share.
Between ups and downs.
Between red and blue.
Between thirst and drink.
And then,
between life and death.

15 September 2016
Prague, Czech Republic

CRITICS (WITH SOME RHYME)

Nothing festoons.
Nothing carouses.
Give me a moment —
of hell and "don't care".
I'm less the fool,
derision is South.
Critics are critics
who shoot from the mouth!!
They can't be the doers
they do scant, then not much.
Shelved in their paucity,
need to garnish a crowd.

Testaceous, the critics
live by their gloat.
Rapacious as parasites,
shrivelled dry, as bland prunes.
Agendas like neons
pulsing bland selves.
Chiding as peons,
their heaving chest swells.
Yet they who create nothing
leave nil in their wake.
Like sump-oil on sand
nothing worthwhile to rake!!

Grum trr picostess artdross
shebl climbzrr honidl techfayz
Assini scheblich brr, brr,
shaupfl amis-like.
Inflominis abi-klep brr
aniti hoosp-self-ego!!!!
Assini scheblick vlugg,
honisti, brr, brr, self-ego.

Shelved in their paucity
they scant outline days.
"Critic" — the word says!
No more to be writ!!
The aim is transparent,
the artist won't win!
Deep ply the shit
like earth on the coffin!
Toss in the negatives!!
Hurling the adjectives!!
The duel is on
between creator and critic!!

No half-time when the critic writes.
No give-an-inch as a reviewer will.
Penultimate triumph, the critic spites.
The artists the victims, jubilant trumpets shrill!!
Nothing to nurture, hold their heads down!
The critic dares sully, the artist must drown!
At opposite ends they parry the duel.
The artist will win! — the critic, death's fool!!
The critics lie on history's fallow fields of inconsequence
supine, their bland print, yellowed page mere nuisance.

Grum trr picostess artdross
shebl climbzrr honidl techfayz.
Assini scheblich brr, brr,
shaupfl amis-like.
Inflominis abi-klep brr
aniti hoosp-self-ego!!!!
Assini scheblick vlugg,
honisti, brr, brr, self-ego.

Most artists don't "cut" much
as history proves
Their potence not potent
nor language, nor concept.
Reviewer discusses, the critic demeans
assuaging limp ego, as a man with Ferrari!!!
They lunge and twist their porous swill
like blackened gargoyles torturing nil!
From first writ louche, the agenda is set
Subjective arrows careen, hurtled and spent.
Then in the bar, the wine, the beer
critic sits sated in ego, knowing critique will appear!

Grum trr picostess artdross
shebl climbzrr honidl techfayz.
Assini scheblich brr, brr,
shaupfl amis-like.
Inflominis abi-klep brr
aniti hoosp-self-ego!!!!
Assini scheblick vlugg,
honisti, brr, brr, self-ego.

29 September 2015
London, England –
8 June 2016
Prague, Czech Republic

SMOKE RINGS

Smoke rings and I are a team,
sometimes —
and sometimes not,
as sometimes smoke rings won't oblige me.

We have an enemy in breeze
or wind.
But when it's still …
what a team!

I'm gentle and they reply
freeing into space;
swirling around themselves
in their short life.

They speed to escape
then slow to dance
almost stopping,
solo, in their performance.

Sometimes they chase each other
in a game of "dare to join".
And when almost caught
trick — and slowly, quickly disappear.

It's even happened — often,
that once free they hesitate
and come again back toward me
as if wanting to have another go.

They're big or small.
Halos of white grey
thinning to size
until gone in their ghostliness.

There's no orchestration,
no choreography —
but deafening silence
in their unique impact.

They leave ordered but grow unkempt
tossing in their buffets;
slandered on their course
from existence to non-entity.

But what joy we'll have,
my team and I, one day.
I'll sit and look around
at a room filled entirely
— with smoke rings.
And only through the holes
around which they all swirl,
will I see anyone come or go;
will I see the walls,
the ceiling,
the floor
or — other smoke rings.

6 January 1976
Vienna, Austria

SPREAD OUT

Butter rubbed the wrong way
burrs —
like armadillo skin;
and runs warm like love.
Sometimes sweats.

To imagine hieroglyphs filled with butter.
Filled with love.
Filled with sweat.
Sweat filled with sweat.

Grab at a moustache of streaked butter
intrinsic on its stuck-on face.
And a peppered balloon
its yellow bleached white ...
then burst —!
Let loose on its universe.

And somewhere a harlequin
with a balloon to burst.
With a face stuck to a moustache;
and a balloon to burst.
All buttered up.

3 January 1976
Vienna, Austria

PERSONAL PERSON

Telephone calls are like that
unless —
you can somehow fit in time
between irreversible beeps
and the inrushing tide
of anticipation.
"Turn down the volume!!"
— "Speak Up"!!
"Isn't the line clear!"
Plastic ear-mouth god
of dispatch, of request.
Sometimes of nothing but talk.
Sometimes of nothing but time-lag.
Sometimes of nothing.

13 December 1975
Vienna, Austria

THE GREEK

There's a plausible impasse in sitting
emptily at a lonely coffee table
(Or should that be sitting lonelily
at an empty coffee table?).
Especially in a crowded café.

My runaway mentors encroach
in camouflaged conspiracy,
surrounded by embittered foes.
The past is ever present
in a present that's just passed;
ever present in
— eroding sculptures
— eroding volumes
— eroding memories

A sugar bowl cajoles its contents
ingrained by its lucid crystals
bayoneted by spoons
indiscriminate in their thrusts
to appease sought-after sweetness,
purveying a refresher course in life.

I throw a glance at eroded sculptures
in the cathedral of my imagination.
I travel instantly in my imagination
and see a portrait of the world
as I remember it
— a bribed tenant
of my own imagination.

As tea leaves leave their swirl
and sink to the bottom
vegetarian dishes promise
a refresher course in life
— an immortal trust account.

And at the next table
sits the Greek —
emissary of renegade card players,
or of a future card game —
savours the melee of maudlin crowds
and plunges his libido into opulent women.

A resonant burp
remarks on his coffee,
and echoes cruel looks
of a slobbering grimalkin
endorsed with the slipslop
of a scrambled egg sandwich
— tarnished a vigorous yellow

The Greek;
a griffin to his own legends
hirsute in his blatant décor
travelling instantly in his imagination
as do I,
and our mind paths meeting
somewhere in Knossos
and beyond.

He contorts an arrogant lip
to smile
secreting thoughts of Knossos
— and I watch him
with pretending-not-to glances
and our thoughts merge
hewn in rampant harmony.

I tarry at my tea
and trill my fingers on the Laminex,
persuading myself to arise and go
and, provoking the gentle jingo
of the stubborn minotaur,
we leave on par
having travelled instantly,
together, to Knossos.

7 – 3 February 1981
Melbourne, Australia

BLIND DATES

Blind dates bring no joy
for blind dates are blind
and respond to voices
at telephone ends
or sudden shocks
at the opening of the door.

Blind dates smell
of embarrassed grins.

23 February 1981
Melbourne, Australia

SUNDAYS

I'm not here on Sundays.
No one is distinguished enough
to partake in unanimous liturgies
hovering over censored spirits and
awaiting the Messianic roll of thunder,
so cueing a multitudinous clap of hands.

Sundays are
a left-over Christmas party
I view from the distance
or less,
as celibate candidates
eke out ecumenical diatribe
for minds of saintly sinners.

I'm not here on Sundays
to recant pious platitudes
or await apparitions
from enthroned arch-clerics,
as saintly sonnets
cruise lofty steeples
to be caught in the mouths
of gargoyles.

Priests plough parodies
of oft-heard formulae,
anointing apparitions
of sacred sentinels
who stand outrageous
— defunct;
yet repeated
in oft-seen icons.

On Sundays
rule me out!
I lunge away from
priestly panacean blessings
pronounced upon prohibited heads
from prohibiting papal bulls once
witnessed by deaf-mute icons.

Welcome Sundays!
You faithful congregants,
fortified by a weeks' atonements
in confessionals
where sins are daily divulged
and excused from the memory
of God.

Prelates juggle collection plates
as fortunes mount
in their minds,
(in Rome's coffers —)
guarantees of impunity; —
such unbeatable value
in perpetual encores
of Sundays.

And all along
eminent eminences
talk in parables
and play rituals with rosaries;
— imagine,
these consecrated worry beads
guarantee impunity.

On Sundays
numerous nuns
dressed in negative habits
glide the wind in muted silences
jostling for privy
in all God's houses.

Lofty descants swarm the steeples
and precisely dissipate into vast silences
as respondents stand dutifully …
or less,
mindful of clutched small Christs
and Amens.

But I'm not here on Sundays
to be aspirated by cleansed ghosts
who regardless, still hold bled biases
of me and my ilk,
to be press-ganged to repentance
for unsummoned sins.
No, not I.

On Sundays
I leave my soul
in annexed cafés,
anointed by waitresses
bearing fresh-coffee offerings.
She from Leningrad
the other, cross-eyed, from Schweiz.

On Sundays, lovers exult life's tryst
taking revenge on love's first sin.
Cossetted from entering church doors,
on sheets wet with
spilt warm juice of cardinal passion
under weekend blankets, hot,
culminating on Sunday night.

Any semblance of time is forgotten
on Sundays.
Only the dutiful have senses of duty,
ministering parables and parodies
to the lonely and fallen
loitering amongst pews in pity,
hoping for eternal salvation
— or at least a room of
spilt warm juice of cardinal passion.

24 February 1981 – 1989 –
27 September 1997
Melbourne, Australia

PRINCE OF BOHEMIA

I am the Bohemian Prince, in my skin.
Incognito, but yet I am.
Claiming the ether
strolling, all routes.
Coronet unseen
judicious my tack
from the lofty bastion, Prague Castle atop.
I can't stop!

Iridescent jewels on canvas and paper
I make.
Stake my claim, denoting my histories,
forging my thoughts
in bursting images
my trumpets roar.

My Bohemia
from where I left to that bottom entity.
But I came back
to the richness of my throne
where I had always grown
and lost and won, and won again.
Sometimes becalmed, then on the rush.
The semaphore called – always –
to return to my coronet
and anoint my head
before dead!

I heed advice but take no fools
and claim no peasants to do this or that
nor turn up my nose, but yes, sniff the air
and boldly stare
and soak my life with no indifference.

The distance is near,
my feet don't bleed.
The ermine cloak hangs in the dank cupboard
waiting … as it's long done,
waiting.

I think far too much, too much of it all,
but no longer on guard or trussed.
Revamped!!
Remade of myself.

My brushes wait — like lances.
Jazz settles, excites the spears of life.
She isn't my wife
but she is my consort
no common retort.

I will go
but not too slow
to place my coronet on my head
again — yes, again.
To place my coronet on my head
despite distractions left and right.
As crystal glasses clink
and little fingers raised — crooked!
As passenger jets contrail overhead
As passengers look down to view my head
The glint of the coronet on my head.

I sit and think as ice blocks melt
Recalling the tossed coin when my fate was dealt.
The spinning crown, tossed by the brothers
In Veletržni those years ago.

Beer, ice cold sweats the glass.
The amber sun sweats my skin.
I am no pretender!
When fate is tossed, it needs to be bent!
The smoke from her cigarette
twists to its height.
The pizza sits, topped with infernal cheese,
stretching.
The yoga class sit,
stretching.
I pass them all on the tourist beat,
stretching.

An insect has fallen into my vodka,
drunk, dead, preserved,
floating to the surface
as my finger slides it out.
Indigo sky.
Cautious silly high heels on cobbles.
Tendentious men at small round tables.
Ghost tours and the costumed guide.
And still my coronet gleams bright.

The English!
The Germans!
Drunk, loud, as if at war,
take over the square
and piss on the church!
Their amber munitions in vast plastic cups.
Loud! Loud! … and louder!
Again …
my kingdom is invaded.
But not!

I watched the elegance of the clouds melding,
drifting,
endlessly.
And one on its own,
the individual.
The one that the eye sees,
examines, reads, wonders,
admires!
For its individuality!
No herd mentality!
And so it is for the Prince of Bohemia!

I look up at the hill.
My coronet is there.
Prague Castle its steward.
Waiting, and … waiting.

Heydrich, evil blond in Hugo Boss black
cut his swathe through history's pack
and probably sized the crown to his head.
Terrible fit!
Not the crown!
His head!!
And without any curse, his end would come anon!

A terrier barks and pulls at the leash,
extendable.
She cuts through the dumpling with finesse,
and sauce!
Do I have some coins, the beggar asks,
seeing my coronet
feeling his privilege,
feeling his moment.

I run my nail against my top lip,
back and forth.
Comfort!
Along the abstract ridges.
As I have since a child.
And still the comfort!
Still, in the ageing man.

The Prince of Bohemia,
the ageing man,
carries his coronet,
heavy,
in red leather case
bespoke!
Step by step his feet intent
Past smothered lovers, oblivious.

So many years, so many jeers
So many struggles, so many fights.
So many yearnings, so much wait.
So little-much time.

They're my favourite
Don't delete.
Don't abscond from lovers' trysts.
Don't retreat from voluminous dreams.
Dust off the past but don't go back.
I journey my road, but look at the mirrors.
My brush ignites its momentous swill.
No fallow image, I make my chance.

Ridicules, so easy, they overfill the grave.
Be proud on your horse
You don't have to, but I am.
He is me and I am he
So read this as you will.

Surging segues strike in convoys.
Tomáš holds to route unnerved.
A handful of brushes, pencils, marks.
The coronet case glowing stoplight red.

The drunken moron trips on cobbles,
even though he knows them well.
His shoulder
hangs inert!
Better him than I.
Speaking of I … I clutch the case.
I could be robbed, or fall, or,
stupidly misplace.

The joker smokes the cigar rolled tight,
grinning the squeal of morbid delight.
Walks through his smoke rings,
the three bells on his head.
I brandish my coronet,
his look left unsaid.

By train to Genoa when I was three.
The coin had been tossed, my fate locked in.
We went, they all stayed.
I lost my Prague, my Europe, my coronet,
for decades.
Even the boat was named "Continental"
steaming us six weeks to the planet's end.
And there I was cooked
but never at home!

Numbers tattooed on various arms.
So many!!
Suspicious! Auspicious! Never mentioned!
Never discussed!
But I knew, from my infant years.
We all knew.
The Fascists! Then Communists!
Down there from the castle
they all marched on
deliberate,
with their new generations.

Intrepid visitor
I came and went!
Belgium, London, Paris, Vienna, Prague
to oh, so many,
then leaving,
depressed!!
Back to world's bottom!
Back to tread water!
Back to ... somehow!

Raphael, Matisse!
From infants to full grown!

Then, ageing
I'm here!
Claiming Prague!
Claiming my coronet!
Prague!
Prince of Bohemia!

The cello plays inside the arch.
The bow across four strings
strikes!
Andante.

Alchemists must still linger in attics.
At some point the Golem takes dark nights
through the town.
Rabbi Löw, his maker, stirs in his tomb,
having met his Maker.

I am my god
I am my Prince
I have to be
No longer an acolyte of anyone,
to believe fantastical vacuous promise!
No religious slurry for me!
But,
Old-New Synagogue stirs my spirit.
Ancient long pennant above the Bimah
now aged pink,
not crimson,
with gold thread star.
Ferdinand III … his gift!

Furtive glances run Charles Bridge
as comic artists steal the cash.
Smetana grimaces at the squeals,
the blackened saints observe, erect.
Sentinel gulls, ordered, aligned,
neatly placed along the rope.
Lanterns … no … lights,
gas lit, everywhere.
Glorious!
Vainglorious!

The trajectory is set
The Castle surmounts.
I am secured.
Quid et quo!
And … maybe, to be continued.

3 – 13 August 2016
Prague, Czech Republic

SMUDGE

Dank!
Smudge!
The air holds a nervous shrill.
Thick humidity deadens all echo.
The smudge appears, there,
on my drawing,
the Rorschach on my hand.

It sits emblazoned,
fully in focus,
screaming loud,
louder than my work.

On the surface,
the paper thick.
Actually –
beautiful smudge!
Very beautiful!
Indigo!
Not so on my left hand,
where it's incised into my handprint,
lacking all delicacy.

I've had smudge before.
Not often but,
often.
A blot even!

It allows me to obfuscate!
Ah, yes!
Use the smudge!
Delve and recreate!
I make the viral critter perform!
Tamed!

So now,
the transmogrification!
The serendipitous thought-play.
The challenge!
Back to control, but
not too much!
Don't use too many neurons!
Don't wait too long!
Coalesce!
Meaning not necessary.
Visual, visual,
visual!
Relate or not.
Or just shape, form,
or colour,
or all!

Sometimes,
but rarely,
another smudge
thwacks the work!
Hard!
Maybe gently!
My fault?
No fault?
The physical stranger appears.

This subterfuge,
this modicum of betrayal.
Coming from nowhere
like a mortar hurled to the flat landscape.
Tumultuous my shock,
inordinate my displeasure,
yet ...
my pleasure.
The surprise will take me to adjacent thoughts
and places.

I have much now to do,
but not much to be done.
Incorporate!
Mitigate!
Smile deftly ... to myself.
Bring out my weapons of creative thought,
then lampoon the happenstance
and claim my potent victory!

Think through the game plan
but not too much.
Toss my grenades, fire my bullets
of shape, form, perhaps colour and content.
Change the direction,
bring all together.
Estimate, laminate,
vibrate with the challenge.

And ultimately,
I do it,
I've done it
and …
All is done!

18 – 22 August 2016
Prague, Czech Republic

THE PAINTER — THE DECADE

Today I am the painter
who cannot work.
For today I am not possessed.

Peer at me
(but not only peer).
Leer at me but,
make me work.
To paint a treatise
of life, with life.

Today I am that painter
a decade on
and sometimes, often, still cannot work.

Don't just mock
nor wipe my brow
servile to my ageing ego;
'tis a decade on now
through oft fallow thoughts
through oft fallow paint.

I glimpse me tight with eyes
as bright as mine once were
and lay to rest on canvas
this, my gem of myopic splendour.
Criticize me!
The story's out —
pilloried on flax stretched cloth!

Hush!
You! You there!
Missive crowds
steeped in social drinking!
Noblesse oblige!
You art-spurred dilettantes!
Don't just mock
nor wipe my brow,
servile to my ageing ego!

Glimpse me tight with eyes
as bright as mine once were.

So, who should cite the annals
of my autumnal prime
if not I?
Who should deal
the coloured fragrances
which glaze my eyes
and my stretched cloth?

I savvy the crowds
I see around
wafting drinks upon
hell-bent speech;
proud vanities secure,
ounce for fluid ounce.

24 February 1979
Reading, England –
24 August 1989
Melbourne, Australia

PENNY ARCADE

At some point in time
I'll find a dime
and kick it so hard
it will fly off the end of my shoe
at a tangent.

But, I presume,
a trick of fate
will have it found again;
by a schoolboy,
a down-and-out,
a housewife,
a shopper,
by someone
— even again
by me —
maybe!?

1978 - 1979
Melbourne, Australia

JSEM ČECH! … CZECH I AM!

Back in London the "Queens" is packed
There's short way forward, a long way back.
Calypso wrangles, contorts to submit
The bottles aligned to tipple a bit.
Bricks glue the row house adjacent to trees
London bonds strong, not bended to knees.
Snowflake so perfect, melts and is gone
Universe's mathematics, but then is frisson.

Ahh, delirium, powers rushed chance,
tosses and tumbles creativity's dance.
All life's rules lie berserk and splayed
leavening anchors, frothing the trade.
Basking no judgements, jilting no spleen,
not living for hope, sweet delirium clean.
Welcome to my mind, the images float
so stubborn, tenacious, I'm born of the goat.

Keep up! Keep up! Life rushes me past!
Keep up! Keep up! My dust beckons fast!
Keep up! Keep up! It's me e'er more alert.
Keep up! Keep up! Never more to divert.
I give myself garlands, plaudits and tributes
I'm drained, I'm spent, drawn pale in sweat
I'm crying, cheeks hot, neglected, bereft.

Do you want a half, or a pint he questions me,
the vodka thrilling my head, thrilling creativity.
Monologue drones numbing my dread
as the sweat drenches my shirt as if I'm being bled.
Look at me drawn of my face, but not gaunt.
Look at me ageing, soon past the jaunt.
All in the pub natter on blithely,
entrenched, sequestered, inured in "Old Blighty".

Grasshoppers sing and leap the frogs.
The fetishists come, traipsing their dogs.
His hat sits square, the felt splays high.
Everyone's wetted, no one leaves dry.
There she is, she tried, to suicide,
but that was then, now she ambles her glides.
Destitute prostitute walks the cobbles
The bit-men pay, she drips her baubles.

Arrogant, I watch, draw and write.
Life's circus plays out, life's seconds held tight.
I the non-smoker, smoke cigar to the ash
claiming the droppings, treasuring the stash.
A little liquid turns ash to my paint
to scrawl ink and ash drawings, my images not faint
No smoke I inhale, I use ash to empower
these drawings I make, they meld and tower.

Should I don a mask of the self-satisfied?
Should I don the mask of money's safeguard?
Should I do the small talk of no real consequence?
Should I nod agreement of no happenstance?
Should I fawn to false friends, swathed in pretence?
Should I not scratch no surface, like them not take chance
Long coats, short coats, armour winter's chill
Most passions end, leaving no thrill.

The coin drops, "cling", on the pavement, no bounce
Glinting winter sun, weighing nary an ounce.
Beautiful women meeting no eye
In Sloane Square nothing much is awry.
Freezing wind cuts my coat, yet still I feel pleasure
So centred in London, my life has no measure.
I draw, I paint, splice collage, write poetry
Nothing and no one negates what is me.

Let's party, scant friends, and revel the life.
Let's party the party, time lost is no wife.
The cold is delicious, for me, not for most
I temper my life, never cold as some ghost.
Let us see how blatant we are and depart
to spit our gumption, debar the niggard.
Matryoshka doll-armies multiply by their threes
Their tight-fitting trios beguile childlike glees.

Nobble the nibbles, loquacious in lust
I don't give a damn, for I will be dust.
I don't matter much, perhaps will leave my scar.
Up ladder, stumble stairs, life's journeys not by car.
Sycophants, hangers-on, I purse hard my lips.
Hope is no heaven, entrancing the Brits.
I watch him sweet-talk, but her boyfriend waits.
Not knowing the endgame, his swell interpolates.

He snorts, and hardens his moments dependent.
Nothing completes, he's Finnish, adjacent.
Inside the cauldron, he's outside the frame.
Pausing for nothing, staring down some grand dame.
His senses blister, erupting mountainous hopes.
He's angry plus dangerous, sleazing mind-fucking gropes.
She floats with the moments, tossing blond Celtic hair.
Revealing tight privacy, rebellious with flair.

I'm absolved of politeness, dissolved of polite onus
I do for myself, not searching for bonus
I watch the world skew-eyed, banish them all
No respect from 'thought friends', now earning their fall.
Should I don a mask of the self-satisfied?
Should I don a mask of money's safeguard?
Should I nod agreement of no happenstance?
Should I fawn to false friends swathed in pretence?

Ah! Let me lighten-up and grin sweet pleasure.
Let us all grasp sweet life with voracious pressure.
Let's grin and glee, these words soon forgotten.
Deliberately stamp on these passions abandoned.
I'm a left-hander, I scrawl to the right.
But I leave potent marks, like the ancient Hittite.
Perhaps someone to find, then my art has certainty.
Like truffles buried, I'm for sniff, and see!

I'm rife with Dada, supinely swimming my head.
Fighting my logic of nouns over red.
Too many conventions I fight to find new.
Too many parameters to destroy, but for nano few.
My images form in serendipitous scree.
Thrust to a surface with nowhere to flee.
Idiot idioms come all together.
Once they are born my images gather.

Mid-career I sit empowered.
Mid-career each new work flowers.
I care nothing for no one's negative humdrum.
The more that there is, the more I gain from.
Judgements are easy, they kindle no flame.
They squeeze their negativity to keep all the same.
Should I don a mask of the self-satisfied?
Should I don a mask of money's safeguard?

Keep up! Keep up! Life rushes me past!
Keep up! Keep up! My dust beckons fast!
With each image I make I push to my limit.
Pursing my lips, I know I will win it.
The tempt of it all is the drug on its course.
And when I'm done I'll be done, no puff of remorse.

24 January – 12 February 2015
London, England

SOMETHING

There is the nothing of everything
— or, is there everything of nothing?
Long grey bitumen streets and paths.
The kilometres!
The vanquished time
of step, after step!
Passing no one
but two or three.
Lifeless life,
but hey ... glorious birds chortle the universe.

You can be miserable in comfort
or ... comfortable in misery.
Wizened folk
like dried prunes in a bowl
look back over shoulders
wishing lost wants.
But hey ... they've purged their trials
and lasted swift eons,
and ... laughed often,
or more.

The guilty claim innocence!
Hic from supped vodka
or whisky … in drams aplenty.
Bridesmaids swivel smiles of grace.
Tresses
Stresses
Noblesse oblige,
as Miles Davis pulses his
'Kind of Blue'.

A monk glides past
hooded in black
naked in sandals
speaks into his Apple
 … to God?

11 June 2019
Melbourne, Australia –
27 September 2019
Prague, Czech Republic

A MIX OF REALITY

Niff-naff … hot is the glass
but quickly grows cold
as vodka crackles the ice cubes
wondrous cracks sluice inside
so quickly find life
till, on the fast melt, they're no more.

Leaves drop on moist ground
and build their dense heap.
Months later in heat, as dead humans do,
leave tracery skeletons.
The instant that was tethered … all gone
but for delicate tendrils, now art.

Young lives saunter past
pulsed, as they are in all times.
Their space oblivious of all care, no regard.
The cigarette lighter sits steel-cold to the touch
awaiting its hot flame, inert object with life.
Balconies empty, lifeless in rows.

Shadow-box! Capitulate! Reveal! Suffice!
"Well — it's funny cos it is!
Awright! Bye!
No woman's werf all dat!
Why bovver?!"
The more she's drinking, the more she's talking!

Sessions are long ... long and filled with widow's weep.
Cold winds cater corpulent crows
eating all hopes with pneumatic confidence.
There's no capitulation here despite fragrance gone.
It's on, and on, and on, and on
till the campaign, at this spot, is over.

Salient winter shadows, long to their end
stamp their presence, slowly on move.
Stark as their presence is their silence
suffice to reveal miniscule stuff of nothingness
scant as holograms purporting a dynasty
S-L-I-D-E with the sun, then — gone!

Dilettantes, champions of nothingness
spew vexatious botherings,
squeal pesky positions of 'emperor's new clothes',
not seen on radars, even as blips!
As in deepest oceans, know nothing of what is
as try their trample, to leave nothing as mark.

Denizens cringe, clamped to small pedestals
fearing uniqueness, fearing all change.
Freeloaders and braggarts purse mottled lips.
Derision spits forth like dog shits on ground.
All in a mob, not-a-one to oppose
fearing drab plumage as apostate.

There's no honey-child in this fetid room!
There's no honey-child in this greyed street!
Beyond their reach in livery
the last Sloane Ranger treads the creep.
High on pretence, coming up for air
with mentally-friendly bundles of vacuous opinions.

Vacuous opinions toss all about.
The women distil all class.
The Uzi is common to protect all from what?
The sauntering cops, conversations their own.
The honey-child rich in love in crooked arm
Settles for nothing, egocentric in claim.

They walk together, but separate they walk.
Pernicious obligation, never more to kiss.
Awaiting denouement, final will be the split.
Their dog wags its tail, loyal to both.
Who is the coward, who has the strength
Champagne pops its cork, the dog trembles, then shits.

Cabs swing corners,
orange their light, or maybe not.
London's clouds paint London's skies
crosscut with aircraft, contrails abstract.
The blind woman swaying white cane feels the ground
seeing nothing of this grand canvas above.

Get to and work ... work!!
Some walk at speed, regulated their lives,
buried in time, trounced in their debts.
Freedoms sacrificed for pounds and pence.
The cassock hides his god's creation
Tight jeans advertise her god's gift.

Libidos run rampant on Kings Road length
lascivious flesh rushes the loins.
Take time, take time, don't put in the pocket.
Claim the time, don't put it in life's bank.
Lust, always young, rushes its course
Though no young pretty looks at aged men.

Older women, luscious in grace
ripened with time, budding their charm.
Trawling the flagstones, deliberate, no haste
Like snails gliding hither, but leaving no trail.
Tight sweaty palms grip airline armrests
Coming into Heathrow, to taste London.

Distant fracas cautions old sot
Weaving his wavers, all blurred and type-cast.
Mutters philosophy, murmurs at life
Holds all his answers, justifying not much.
Lone fox, audacious, on evening's run
Red fur coat bristles, devouring all found.

The dealer deals, the spruiker spruiks, Oyster card beeps.
All conforms but the artist doesn't!
All for everything, but maybe not.
True creative statement burns for posterity, maybe not.
The pulse runs quick, excited by marks
As images coalesce, as poems' words collide.

Statements of 'confidence' advertise brands
worn emboldened, but emboldening nothing.
Like uniforms of intent, scant symbols of corporates
emblazon for others to validate selves!
Not much to offer, needing a tag
wearing the big price, vacuous full scant.

Mustard on fat, dog shit underfoot
Street cleaners brush, then trundle their carts
Meet up in convoys, it's back to their base
Their day's at its end, their swagger complete.
Dogs shit again, chewing treat sticks
Abstract dollops await the sole!!!

Tar-boy works the steaming cauldron
Rusted buckets heaved to roof
Georgian houses, terraced, united
Blue sky breaks through as the season turns.
The down-and-out is out, not down
Winter survived, her frail bones warm.

Where do all the conversations go?
Their sonic sounds in waves replete.
Arguments, passions, debates, dismissals,
crescendos, whispers, fillips, shrills.
The egos, betrayals, demands, the offences,
the nurtures, apologies, manipulations, control.

Sybil still plies her nonsense trade.
Eons have passed but nothing much changes.
Hercules' muscles … pumping his gym
vacuous brawn beneath vacuous brain.
Brick layers beautifully point reddish bricks.
Surgeons knit to claim time from time's death.

Goya's witches still powerfully dance
Rubens' Rubenesques still bloat to the full
Hoards cascade the galleries' doors
Knowing nothing of much, but have-to must-see
Selfies and selfies, to prove they've been there
But where it all is are ticks on the map.

Harried and hurried, their frowns etched deep.
Sanguine lads posture, their lives erect.
They know no boundaries, no, no, not yet.
Tousled hair, their fingers comb.
The older man covets someone's wife.
Awaiting his foray, but fearing rebuff

Discord of moments meet the rhythm of time.
Hyacinths, bluebells, and daffodils burst forth.
Carpeted perfumes trounce British air.
Free of expenses, rich fragrance enthrals.
Next week comes, and next month goes.
All's so quick in London Town.

Like caryatids, spruikers swivel Kings Road shop steps.
Vacuous their beckoning, hideous lies entreat.
She's black, she's brown, she's white, she's she.
She's Muslim, all covered, her beauty unseen.

17 February – 25 February 2015
London, England

DON'T

Curious!
We never see people die in the streets.
Nor on the paths,
nor the shops,
on a daily basis.

Don't sleep!
Don't shut your eyes!
Don't shut down your awakening!

Stethoscope echoes the beat
of life's drum.
Loud!!
— but a distant murmur.
Lucifer's tangle claws a clutch
with eyes blind to all beauty.

Undertakers wait.
Play cards
in their faux sympathy parlours.
Pallbearers pace their boredom,
till,

the phone rings!
The business of death,
life's certainty,
resumes.

Lucifer chuckles.
Church bells toll long.
Vacuous promise of eternal life
stays dark!
The box, the hole,
the thud of shovelled soil!
DON'T sleep!!

13 August 2016
Prague, Czech Republic

THE AMERICAN

The buggers, the luggers
the spurious others.
She leans on left elbow
parading her flesh.
Dyed apricot hair
chancing vague catch.
Vamping her lashes
extensions enmesh.

Tight faded jeans
ripped at her knees.
Pert her string top
so black into night.
As twigs in a tree
supporting its trunk,
she swills white the wine
her body on heat!

There's din in the quietude
shouting through silence.
There's stirring of life
deep in dark crypt.
She passes my glass
to endanger … more wine.
He watches slant-eyed
as erected, erect.

In his dark, a blind knave taps.
On the sniff, on the game.
Master of senses
and savvy his quest.
Parades his demeanour
as if peacock's feathers.
She gawks and inhales
then, dismisses his space.

She actions her drawl
from some place south.
"Ah don't get this kerntry,
but mah gawd it's nice".
She vamps again,
her lashes flick.
Refills my glass
to the rim.

She phones her boss.
She's sick today.
Can't go to her job,
the doctor ordered!
Speckled dragons float her mind,
her distant fantasies pervade.
Decades collide as so do mine.
Perhaps she looks better naked!

Somewhere in our potent silence
a tap drips.
Somewhere in our potent silence
her left goes right!
She fidgets.
Shakes her drifting head —
in desire to realign lost memory moment
to prequel.

I stir, now awake.
The abstract dream dissolved.
Dark is outside, lit by measured lamps.
Lit by skewed memories vague.
My studio beckons, siren on rock.
"Biggles" flies in from my youth.

18 June – 2 July 2018
Prague, Czech Republic

PASSION-PORTFOLIO

I keep a passion-portfolio;
Seething/Obliging/Suspect
on my back seat
on a winter hill.
So diplomatic in a portfolio.

A convoy of back seats
blanketed by reclining discarded lovers.
Discarded lovers separated
by bucket-seats
by armrests.
Breathless,
sometimes aged.

They sit
and wake in sequences
like stills from a movie.
And as I take them from my portfolio
they blush at their selection.
The hazed grey of their discard
momentarily furnaces the blush.

I don't always need them in a portfolio.

Colognes/Perfumes/Scents
all jest — tempts in their bottles.
The beckoners of lovers and of discards
again wake, in sequence.
I keep my passions in bottles.
Discards —
so known and expensive
in known and expensive bottles.

Occasionally they repeat themselves.
Stir —
in moments of weakness;
for moments of weakness;
of moments of sequence.

We meet at my portfolio
and I stare at their perplexity
of want, but can't.
Again they blush;
then I blush
and I am seduced by the blush
for only then — seeing and sensing them again,
I remember —
I too have been a discarded lover.

5 – 6 January 1976
Vienna, Austria

THE EXHIBITION

Hush.
You! You there!
Missive crowds
steeped in social drinking!
Noblesse obliges!
You art-spurned dilettantes.
Don't just mock
nor wipe my brow
servile to my ageing ego!

Glimpse me tight with eyes
as bright as mine once were!

So who should cite the annals
of my autumnal prime
if not I?
Who should deal
the coloured fragrances
which glaze my eyes and hang
on my stretched cloth?

I savvy the crowds
I see around,
wafting drinks
upon hell-bent speech,
proud vanities secure,
ounce for fluid ounce.

The artist comes.
Man-Friday from his studio
trussed naked on these gallery walls,
trussed doubt for savaged doubt.
The artist dares
where devils bare their hoary chests!

Almost total, almost bare-naked,
exposed to all
I'm laid open, by will,
for all to see, leer, mock, explore
— at times to admire, like, embrace.
Trite — this tryst I try to write.

Engage me they do
in their vicarious plot
to know, (they think), the artist.
To gloat to all that they'd met me once
as years default.
To then say in a future null and void
they could a bargain have bought
in times thence, for the price of a toy.

The crowds then swell, then thin, then out.
They'd worked the room, drinking free swill.
And I stand surrounded by my suite of time
nary a red dot to sustain my life.
And, as lights snap out
I down some plonk, and gird resolve
cheating the cheaters with my hell-bent!

The studio plays its triumphant tune
Reverie, nonplussed of all I am.
Mordant gallery caring not
The artist, me, slugged across its walls
for them, meaningless nothing
all changed if they're bought.

Down Alice's rabbit hole
I question and wrestle
spliced to the canvas
the slurp of lush brush.
Matisse and Raphael, (no not the artists),
my progeny wondrous, can survey my stored stock
when I am buried in body, not my testament.
My ordinations are penned by my brush.

Always the optimist, I rattle and prattle
my life's arrogance and journey
I cleave from my core.
When no more of me is left
some they will find me
and spectate at this man,
surmising my template
they'll chafe abstractions
my moments of yore.

Nothing is left and nothing matters.
God of myself, I've benched my mark.
Who dares can look, who doesn't won't
The glut of my life … I'll leave an ark!

5 August 1989 Melbourne, Australia
20 September 2014
- London, England

COFFEE SHOPPE

I looked obliquely and saw them both
Raise the cups to the mouth; in unison
At separate tables, oblivious of each other
And sipped once the hot coffee, their
both right hands replaced the cup; in unison.
Picked up bothersome cigarettes,
fuming rasping smoke
And with right hand placed it in the mouth
— in unison.
Inhaled and blew out acrid fumes; together.
Looked at me and looked away
one man, one woman choreographing
in this coffee shoppe.

1 June 1989
Melbourne, Australia

WHAT I'VE DONE ... I'VE DONE IT!

I remembered where the light switch was.
I clawed my way through sanity.
Thus and then I left the shores
To London West and East.

What I've done ...
I've done it!

Timorous clues remain of me.
I'm pardoned in folly
with nought to repent.
Sitting at a pub's table
Now and then alone.
Now and then not.

What I've done ...
I've done it!

I've made so much work
since I left those shores.
High on life I cannot stop
as more and more my work explodes!

My creative rushes are no bull!
There's no basket to be found in the bull rushes
No basket of gifts hidden but to be found
For me no parlay in what I do
For me no parlay in what I create
Work, gorgeous work, surprises me

What I've done ...
I've done it!

Leave me to rest and take a breath,
at Tryon Street in gracious "Queens".
Swill a dram, or two or three
and juggle my head with creativity.

Never still this head of mine
Crammed imagery waiting to burst!
I'm my god to myself awaiting no shrine
No promise of later supplication.
Not servile to their "Death's promise"!

What I've done ...
I've done it!

No "Amens" for me to leave behind
No promises or saviours will me appease
My work, my work, my work I leave
And they will judge, disseminate
or ... cast aside
And I, in the earth for eternity shall hide

What I've done …
I've done it!

What I've done …
I've done it
and left behind
the thoughts of my life.
But … I've left behind!

What I've done …
I've done it!

21 April 1992
Melbourne, Australia –
9 September 2014
London, England

HA! HA! HA! HA! HA!

Hell bent mystics fart around
espousing thoughts and threats.
Flush nonsense rants under beehive hats
from self-made priests
with huge bank accounts,
tax-free now they have their numbers.
The needy fill the doom.
Altars spewing tongues of promise
sucking the torn insanities.
Handing souls their hopes in death
their coins to buy jubilant paradise space.
The rants, the rants, the rants!

Oh god of myself
I've let me loose
so long ago from any promised noose.
Self-serving bigots prey the flesh.
No proof of promises required to acquit
nor demanded or sought
but pledged for cash.
Croupier prelates will place your bets
and spin your life from red to black
and you are a winner till death's door slams
you'll win the nothingness of evermore.

Go to them then, go to them
and seek promised salvation.
Hand them your cash
for death's safe haven.
And when you are buried
entombed under tree
will you claim a refund
from death's guarantee?
There's nothing to promise, there is nothing there.
Who's ever come back from death's
finite corsair?

Did you just linger in gutters so vile
lest live your own person
and make it worthwhile.
Meat on the cleaver
bones under cement,
the ordained count sweet cash —
is that money well spent?
Soothsayers, ordained, nutters or champs
all promise dank words, with no gods' stamp.
They're not quite dead, nor ever come back
to prove a morsel of anything,
it's all clap trap.

I can write my own bible, stand up and preach.
I could earn enough money and be some gods' leach.
I could preach some salvation and explain a missed train,
or a death or a marriage or when nothing's to gain.
I could hold my hand out and grease my dry palm
or promise you life without doing harm.

I can do it for nothing and teach you to see
that you are your own god, over a
beer or a tea
You need nothing but self, need harbour
no doubt
You have your one life, hold your head up
and shout.
I am who I am!!! with all that life brings
and don't need false promises, devised by
human beings …
who are the same as me but try to
wield power
over those vulnerable, who's
life's a bit sour.

And when you're down there
plucked to the bone -
or ashes scattered
whereabouts unknown.
Scrambled as eggs
or boxed as death's gift,
back to the universe
it's stardust replete.

I find it so boring to write of all this
of gods invisible who never appear
of liturgies and texts which want all to die
before reaching salvation in judgements and sky.
The stories are great and a wonderful show —
but to live by their tenets, oh no, no, no!

Who were the secretaries who wrote it all down
with hammers and chisels on stones from the ground.
With lightning speed as words tumbled out
as detached shadows carousing about
to record gurus' pronouncements for religions' clout!
With blah, blah, blah – mine's better than yours
Let's solve it all with religious wars!!
And endless gods ever insist
never showing themselves
so, this all desists.

I am god of myself
I've let me loose
So long ago from any promised noose.
Proved by nothing I rule me alone
My paradise is now, not when I'm bone.
I live gentle in London fulfilling my life,
Not waiting for death, and no afterlife.
Ha! Ha! Ha! Ha! Ha!

20 – 1 September 2014
London, England

THE PIMP

A sleuth slimes past
re-glancing his just previous moment
and allowing his shadow to catch up.
No comic of humour or comical twit
yet resisting no belly laugh
at seeing, perceiving, the next fellow
obliged in his rigid embarrassment
of voluminous nudity.

And such voluminous nudity,
repeated
and hanging pegged
in an empty dressing grown
— his empty dressing gown;
an icon
echoing his voluminous nudity.

The sleuth slimes past
daring his glance
then pledging his stare
at the next fellow,
once laudable of birth right
yet here ignoble
bar his sodden kitty
of touted sweaty notes.

The fellow;
tufts of tribute for hair
weed from his head;
grinning the gleaming nugget
of a gold tooth.
An envoy of sorts —
wizened monarch of bestial parlours,
a suzerain
condescending to harlots' grins.
An envoy of sorts
with a salary to prove it.

Staccato speech in italics
slang slurs from his mouth
trembling in financial excitement
and cascading in tiers
of voluminous nudity
echoed in the pendulum
of a burning yellow globe
pivoting the voluminous shadows
of the room.

The sleuth slimes past
bereft of harlots
fondling his shadow,
cherishing translucent afterthoughts
of the next fellow
— bribed despot
of incredulous tenants —;
re-glances the icon
and smothers a belly laugh
— and disappears

14 April 1980 – 14 February 1981
Melbourne, Australia

HIERATH

I watched a man die this morning.
The last breath heave and none to spare
embezzled in the festival of nothingness.
The "Is", is "Was", but now I have watched
a one-way transition of two realities.

I cradled his head
I gave him air
from weakened mask,
no intake pulled.
Sallow body
and no one cared
but I, in my youth
I fumbled alone.

All ran helter-skelter
from the strife —
fearing the guilt
of taken life.
Hierath alone —
long last gasps drawn.
Chiding life's presence
servile to their care.

Hierath died
oh so, so alone
But for me his head held
I've always atoned.
Too young to demand
was I to insist
all who knew
must never desist!

So alone in his death
no parental kin.
Only but I
could oxygen spin.
No pressured pumps
to salve from death,
Hierath parted
to meet with Seth.

I'll join him lonely
we both astray.
Only he will know
what I did that day.
Hierath spilled
his sputum green
Agnostic or religious
he vented his spleen.

I've lived consummate life
and drenched my bag.
His posthumous soul
I've always dragged.
— in Memoriam
And ... only 30!

17 March 1975
Vienna, Austria –
23 September 2014
London, England

THE RHUBARBARIAN

Probably he was sired from driftwood
or maybe he was some-such graft.
The glistening bald head televising
motifs of chiaroscuro.
Customary constipation bubbled somewhere within
the faded pre-washed jeans.
Looks about
sucks his bottom lip
and seasonally snorting eloquence
from his beer-blushed nose
(stuffed with snuff lifted from Fleet Street)
he sniffs the blonded milk in a rip-top carton.

Confession was slow this morning
but when his turn came he'd told of
non-existent sins to the Father.
A daily ritual this
— gestured for the daily gossip
of the cloisters.
Besides … he wasn't Catholic.

In the pissoir
he'd farted as he passed the toilet lady.
The least she could do was hold it for him
if she wanted a tip.
He wondered what sort of woman she was
— what qualifications
to work in such vestibules of power,
amid the philosophized graffiti and such
expulsions of energy.
Why tip a privilege?

Back here
he'd wanted to read a borrowed copy
of "The Source"
but instead read "The Times" — (airmail edition)
— from January 16th.
He'd read it often of course,
but now as it was eleven months old
he considered it a collector's item
— so it should be read often
— of course.

He pours the milk remains
into the instant coffee
— dissolved by hot coppered water.
Sips — and sucks his bottom lip.
Questioningly
he bites the dry croissant
(which has been lying on the sink)
and chews it deliberately with impeccable teeth
— as a fly rests at a milk spill.

At the windows
(after three deliberate strides)
he looks down on Rue de Saint Quentin.
Seasonally hot steam fans
from his pulsating nostrils
— smashing silently at the glass
and he watches sprinkles of people
stepping down into the yawn of the Metro
— and sucks his bottom lip.

Throws a quick glance back
at his favourite chair
– the only one (a Club piece)
and when there, slumps in, and
fingers the fray on the right-hand arm
and tugs taught the loose braid of weave
which slips to longer length.
Then, with impulse
grabs his high ox-blood boots
pulling them over his jeans
— and sits

Later, he picks up the receiver of the telephone
(long disconnected for some obvious reason)
and, as if expecting to be surprised
dials
— but stops at the second last number
— there is still no dial tone
and besides, he dislikes telephones.
They're so impersonal …
(and who would he ring anyway)
  … and comical.
He'd watched people through windows
talking and gesturing to a mouthpiece.

He sucks his bottom lip.
Inhales —
and tenors three bars from "Salome"
then dum-dee-ums
and with frenzied arms
conducts and hums
— before abdicating.
And, as a final tribute
clicks his tongue against impeccable teeth
— and leans against the sink
— startling the fly.

Looks at the ceiling —
he disrespects the Russians.
If the system's so good, why fear
letting that scientist go for his Nobel Prize!
Wouldn't he want to go back
— if the system's so good?
He'd seen his face in "PARIS MATCH"
and now he sees it again on the ceiling
— which needs to be repapered or painted.

His lips thin and extend to a smile.
Once in Singapore he'd been asked
(... by a Buddhist priest,)
to bow three times to the altar
(holding a joss stick in each hand)
before being allowed to take a photo
— of the same altar.
He doesn't recall having seen flies
— in Singapore.
And he still had hair then.

He shudders a cold shiver down his back
— pleasant in the heat.
Turns
and strums his nails along the sink corrugations;
and mellows —
thinking of loves loved
and wonders when he will see her again
— all of them.
The floods of memories, powerful and painful
upset him, though not really.
Bites a fingernail.

He'd once created a sculpture
and looks at it on the veneered table
standing over the maquette.
The maquette married to the bronze
— but ignores both.
Instead, careens a brush first to paint
then into the canvas
— after all he is a painter.
It was a long time since he'd been drunk.
Some time ago.

Above —
nebulous haze hangs like haze should,
muffling the sun,
like a rebuke to the weather, whatever it is.
But only a camouflage.
He likes weather;
its honesty — its distortions
but always there.
And he could enter it or leave it.

And extends himself to full height,
(the more-than-not added by his boots).
Curtails a glance at the painting
and manipulates on a high neck sweater
— deliberately.
Walks out the door
(to friends)
and sucks his bottom lip
between impeccable teeth.

7 – 11 December 1975
Vienna, Austria

GHOSTY

There's an agnostic ghost
romping its journey.
It takes it easy,
only back on Thursday.
Don't know what it's thinking about
there's no doubt about that.
It mooches about
not caring for walls.

Not fat, nor skinny
not high nor low.
With a grin —
as only a ghost will grin.
The Scot orders a whiskey
heavy in kilt, light in the dram.
He has a reputation for being aloof,
scorns the English for stealing the throne.

Ghosty hovers above the stool.
No need for food, but whiskey's good.
The bottle levitates to pour the more,
but never to be the drunk!

No need for religion.
No tea leaves to read.
No fuss or preen.
No mirror to stare.
Everything's porous,
no bumps or bruises.

A hoary codger flays his stick
as if Errol Flynn with his sword.
He's seen the grin and felt cold chill,
mutters, to get ghost from his path.
Grin widens.
All suddenly gone.

The breadth of the world is Ghosty's to play.
Segueing.
Eavesdropping.
Never sloppy.
Never commercial.

Sometimes bumps — (can't bump) —
into ancient ghosts.
All share the grin
of their nothing to care.
There's nothing to miss,
it's always all to be had.
No bag, nor suitcase.
No sore back.

No plane bookings.
To hell with passports and searches!
All done at life's end.
Buried or burnt —
forget it.
It's over!
Outta here!

The duck, meerkat, know nothing of time.
They don't even know of poem nor rhyme.
What's "Mona Lisa" with eternal smile
glued to the canvas,
fixed!

Tourists —
search through menus
to fill growling stomachs.
The ghost remembers
but he has no need.
Ten thousand minutes later
it commands splayed grin —
wide.

Ha! ... Ha, ha!
Squeal the joke.
Slam no lid at life's death door.
Tighten no fist,
swill that drink!
Your ghost-self awaits
with impervious grin.

I write all this
with joyous acceptance.
Why rattle with fear
of the only definite?
Despite all that,
I don't believe —
in ghosts!

24 – 25 September 2018
Prague, Czech Republic

ODE TO MYSELF

Catch the ball
but let it drop
to roll and find its place.
There is not much there
but sand.
And yet
the ball claims its space …
as a ball fills the empty gallery,
lying ethereal
at any point on the floor.

Did you ever think of a secret
from four decades ago?
As the waitress strikes
the tray on her knee.
As the wind rustles evergreen leaves
after crossing the world.
As the peon dreams
the same dream unfulfilled.
As you sat on the wicker chair
at the same reserved corner table
of the bar.

You learned to fly,
to take off and land,
alone, in secret,
fulfilling a dream.
The man —
the artist, the pilot,
poet even!
The stuff of your life!
Oh! All that stuff!
And yet — determination fulfilled!

The wind always blows
after crossing the world.

Shoot the breeze!
But why shoot at all?
They shoot all the time
in the U.S. of A.
"God's Own Country"
they claim in arrogance.
That god, sanctions the gun.

Bang! Rat a tat, tat! Bang, bang, boom!
More school kids dead!
Again, and again!
God's given right acclaimed!
Then silence!
All await each toll!

The wind always blows!
Clouds slide their freedom
swooning on currents.
Crossing the world.

Oh yes
you learned to fly.
And oh yes,
you easily cry.
Your life foretold on the toss of a coin
Trumped by your father.
Lost by his brother!
From communism
to some evolving democracy!
The deed was done
for some decades.

Life's tortured refugee.
Stories, belongings,
ingrained by your father.
The serendipitous toss
will arrive, full circle.

Did you ever think you would meet her,
so different?
In London town.
In Trafalgar Square.

Did you ever think you'd laugh again?
And again, again
from then till the end!
Do your children know
their father
the clown
who she brought back to life
to mirror your soul
to spin with her,
through life.

Do your children know
who you really are?
Were they interested
to honour your history?
To regale in your stories?
To wander in your life?
To astound at your daring?
To honour your decisions
for what you gladly gave up.

Give me a vodka
to salute a life lived.
Covet sweet essences
of each tick of the clock.
Sit in the corner
and draw moments of lives
with tears stymied
with what's learned with age.

Oh, to have known all this then
as winds have crossed the world
then gone to some nowhere, forgot!

22 – 23 November 2018
Prague, Czech Republic

WHACKY THURSDAY

The day was strange.
I had to think.
From the eve before —
to set the alarm,
to time the cab,
to take the necessities,
to fall asleep,
all for the next morning.

I awoke to the tune,
though slept so little.
Torrid summer heat
negating the night.
Tormented loud drunks
enslaved the street.
Mix that with the heat
— oh, the heat.

So, into the cab
and off for the resonance!
An MRI to determine my head.
To breach my skull.
Pert nurse positions headphones.
The grill tethers my face,
as in "Silence of the Lambs",
I stare the outer.

The headphones 'bookend' my head!
Pulses pulse
different speeds
assorted frequencies
nascent pitch like dance-club halls,
beguiling.
And then the silence
like death expectant.

It's my head, my head
not yours for the take!
I own it!
Connected to my neck!
Connected to the rest of my 'is'!
Not for your take!
But by now the pulse-beats
give me reassuring time.

What will they find?
What will they see?
What do they know
that I don't know?
Do I matter
if only for me?
Do I matter
at all for them?

White in their garb
as if Hollywood heaven.
I lie on my back
encased in a tube.
The rays disarray
my brain from my skull.
Like Mickey Mouse
my life is frame by frame!

I lie on my back,
grill on my face,
not allowed to move,
yet my pulsating chest moves!
But now in this instant
I enjoy the sounds!
The rhythm,
the beat, the ups and downs.

Do I matter in this tube,
as if catacomb deep,
cleaving me
ornate in surgical gown,
as some dead monk propped in catacombs?
Do I really matter?
Numbed to strange beat sounds
fighting sleep's drift.

I can't indulge to the drift!
I might move!
I may toss with the tempo!
Or snore!
Or snort!
Or giggle replete!
Or shudder
then jerk to awake.

I'm comfortable in this tube
but want to get out!
Enough is enough!
Who's having the fun?
These comic strip images
frame by frame
telling the story
of my phantom brain.

Now nearly an hour on
surely the end is soon!
Sudden sedated fear
of shards of "what if"?!!
Well, yes, what if —
my life cascades
from the pulsed findings
of my sliced brain?!!

And yet —
I drift to sleep
so relaxed,
to the rhythm of changing sound.
But then awake
as mustn't move!
As those in the control room
watch — and peer, at imagery of my core.

It's enough!
Surely enough!
To clear or designate me
to vagaries of unknowns.
Yet still calm
in this pleasure of experience.
Then … everything stops,
confounding my wait.

The click of the door.
Padded footsteps approach.
A button must-pressed
to slide me to the world — again!
Headphones removed
I slowly arise
and back to a room
to dress.

Belongings gathered
I sit the wait,
my partner by my side
concerned.
A CD I'm given
as if some gift
of those images ... and a report.
So, here I sit and write — all clear!

T.E. FANTL
3 – 8 November 2018
Prague, Czech Republic

HEART!

Oh, the heart!
The boom, boom, boom!
Keep on beating!
Do your magic!
You little thing
of quintessential power!
Sparking each pulse
of life's next second.

Some call it the "ticker"
as it counts down time.
The throb of existence
on readying the soul
to smile,
to think,
to love or hate,
to pulse the life force of everything.

Oh, what a beat!
Oh, what a treat!
To laugh the joke.
To taste the wine
To lust the sex
and beat the delight!
To feel the cloth

and overpower the ills!
Course through the veins
to replenish life's force.
Taste the delights
that ply the tongue.
Sidle through life
ignoring an end.
Awake in the morning
after the rest, but ... heart hasn't!

Heart beats on
through life's loads dropped!
Through torpid states!
Nightmare dreams!
Ingenuous accusations!
Drunk to the fall!
Aircraft in turbulence drop!
And ... delicious skies!

Three billion beats
in the average life.
But don't start to count now.
Time's running out!
Emotions!
Oh emotions —
play the other hand
of Takotsubo cardiomyopathy!

Slow!
Slow yourself down!
Savour life and time!
Next beat is the gift!
Next second — ditto!
Whatever you sequester, or don't,
there's only heart
there's only beat … until not.

Who's on the left?
Who's on the right?
Who is an ally?
Who is a foe?
Who is the pauper,
refugee or disabled?
Who wins the final bucket-load rich
when heart beats last beat?

Perfect design
this fist-size muscle
of ultimate beauty,
beating life's life
to the prescient end!
Ah! The end!
Who knows when?
Who knows where?

Beat!
Beat!
Boom the boom!
Sometimes silent.
Sometimes pounding!
Sometimes racing.
And … at the last second …
no time to regret … over and out!

9 – 13 November 2018
Prague, Czech Republic

PULL ON YOUR TIGHTS!

Pull on your tights!
Dim the lights!
Winter's a-coming
to squelch snow
and, slip.

Sun will glint on blue snow.
Mulled wine, hot, will mist dry air.
There'll be holes in the ice
where fishers dare.

Hot breath sprays.
Jesus comes to life —
if you believe.
Or perhaps … to deceive.
Remember the child with gifts.

Buy, buy now, before it's too late!
Aircraft will fly —
if de-iced.
Smoke will hang
till breeze disperses.
Sound thuds to silence,
no echo nor bounce.
Hooray!!

There's a duvet to snuggle.
Body warmth to infuse.
Sales at the stores
to buy what's not needed.

There'll be those who scurry to warmer climes.
There'll be those who savour thick soups —
sublime.
To coorie in merriment.

15 October 2018
Prague, Czech Republic

ABSURD WITH TABASCO SAUCE

He had nerve!
Prodding a wink of concession
yet always in a hurry.
He'd come from a gene of blind courage
yet — gentle with magnetism.
Umpteen rebuffs
and umpteen small tariffs for tolls.

Continuous sniffs through "Bed and Breakfasts";
monstrous fortunes of VATs and taxes.
And yet present persuasions pivot
in a Bloody Mary,
absurd with Tabasco sauce
Absurd with erubescence.

But now I've drunk!
And so let me read you of other things;
of adulation yet frivolity.

I once thought profound thoughts
but now I seek a leaden reprieve;
and strangely, I recall launderettes
so universal
almost contrived
almost ribald.
And always I finish up
with an odd sock
— extra! (more or less).

Through supermarkets
I'm swept past prostrate packers;
massaged by queues and trolleys;
to the dictum of the register
vomiting numbers,
jettisoning tallies
— and gratefully, out!

This London —
this mutation of a city
pretentious in its reality
and, all the realities
ensconced in its focus.
Such a milieu of the world
and truly, <u>THE</u> British Museum.

She laughed as she had to
at my having blown a tyre
for the third time last week.
At my running out of petrol
for the fourth time in four days.
Leaning back, she
— just laughed, as she had to.

Still,
be that as it may.

I grew absurd with Tabasco sauce
and gunned courage
and professed my love
— and by God, I feel better now
(despite the slick of that spilled sauce
burning the fade of my jeans).

2 April 1976
Bath, England –
19 June 1976
London, England

LIDO DI CLASSE

Old women;
long soured of flawless beauty;
long cracked as the lizards
aloof on balmy rocks.

Old women;
knee-high stockings strangling bulges of flesh
uglily exposed
below un-glorious pantaloons,
beneath restless skirts.

Old women;
Adriatic old women
ebbed in curiosity as are the ebbing waters
tasting the sands.
Old women — as their mothers before them.

I saunter and stop.
Another shell swirls, wet,
and stops.

A dog sniffs
at the gnarled feet of old women.
I call but I am ignored.
An Italian dog responds to Italian,
even dialect,
as in Austria dogs respond to German.

Old women,
the same, haul in the curiosity of their nets
gossiping in gestures, crackling in voice
I saunter and ... kick the Adriatic.

4 September 1977
Ravenna, Italy

AGO

Don't you think it's windy today?
After all the wind is blowing,
and your eyes are strewn with tears
and the clouds above are rushing by.
And like the wind you pass what you want to
stopping only to preen yourself
in occasional mirrors,
and adjust your dialects of fashion.

I've listened to the dictum of rain
on cathedral roofs.
I've seen it sliding wetly down tiles of slate.
I've turned a redundant eye
and cocked my head
to see it always there overhead;
the Gothic gargoyle
beautiful in its ugliness,
spewing cascades onto far below.

If I'm found in folly,
pardon me.
You passed me by at a point in time
when I wasn't ready for your encounter.
But we tied down the sun in
half-filled meadows
by the back door.
And postponing a little,
become two scoundrels
on the same wavelength

18 December 1977 – 21 February 1979
London and Reading, England

THE SAGE

He sits encapsulated —
a sage —
enwombed in the familiarity
of the café,
in its warmth;
sucking thoughts through warm spaghetti;
and all around
watching lips mouth words
in never ending sequence
but for breath pause,
for thought pause.

Copious pickets swirl outside,
swirl around.
The un-unionised knave
chalking up concrete
as harassed harridans cavort,
balancing staccatos of
their carrier bags,
passing walls of half-written stock
and the half-painted life
of graffiti.

An incongruous dwarf
waddles his entrance
swathed in incongruous chic
of lavender,
and with a flannel effort on his head,
(an excuse for a beret):
No cherub
but rather a self-professed chevalier
of some unadopted army.

He was stencilled into life
to collaborate
and now sits encapsulated —
a sage.
A sage, tethered in his thoughts
infringing on the table
at which he sits,
and the soggy pestiferous puffs
back out of his pipe.

I watch him,
looking at myself.
I've been endorsed
and I think of my father.
When you look at me
do you see my father?
But I grapple!
I grapple myself,
I grapple the sage
and I grapple my father.
But don't give me back my gutter!!

26 February 1979
Reading, England –
29 March 1980
Melbourne, Australia

ENTRE CÔTE

Do you realise what death is?
It's a finality!
The end of an entity!
And I could be gone from you tomorrow
and you from me
and both of us from them all
and from it all!

You say you gear yourself to that possibility.
But what if I actually went — or one of the others?
Will you accept it? —
Can you just leave me as I had left you?

I'm with you now, so keep me.
I love you now, so love me.
I want you now, so want me.
I need you now, so need me.

Be certain of your certainties
and undulate with the unknowns.
Grasp, like I do, what for today I have got!

12 May 1977
Perry Green, England

BABBLE

Tyres hot, soft ...
boiled to sweating tarmac
noisily "smick!!"
on black trace to town.
Like a roll of liquorice
already chewed,
sweet, hard to swallow
the ride.

Turgid the tumble weeds,
then wind drops, gazumped!
Flat as a saucepan
its heat bloats vague mirage.
On, god's sake on —
bring up the town!
Heat numbs his near sleep.
Slits betray where once were eyes!

The docent slides
the latch of old.
She sits herself down
knees slight apart.
Ennui, her monotone,
he slaves to his chair,
decides to cough

as alarm clock to wake.
He continually nods
his answers.
"I know! I know!" in rote,
wading through her fog of thoughts.
Prosaic his boredom
as military orders!
Holds, breathy his moment
— smiles!

Slow, so slow,
old water wheel turns.
Two centuries lasting
with only repairs.
The brook gurgles same babbles
as always has done.
Mordant in history
scant little has changed.

Tab — now I remember,
Tab was his name.
Hers I didn't hear —
and nor does it matter
so "he" and "she" will do
through this gist.
On and on the jukebox plays!
On and on old vinyl's drop!

Oblique
she sits from left to right.
Left elbow supporting
her muttering head.
Metallic green fly finds its place.
Six legs splayed on her shoulder.
She drones on ... he fakes a cough.
Bored too, the fly is — off!

The sun's long late shadows
arc the room.
Waiter scans
— no change.
Tab levers to up,
off to the toilet.
She forces slits to her eyes,
closes, babbles on.

16 – 18 July 2018
Prague, Czech Republic

ON

Write to me with the puerile pen.
The chicken from egg will rise again.
Hoisted masts for happenstance heroes.
Toss the bottles to festive smash!

Crowd the banks on the riverside.
Claim the castle surmounting the hill.
Deride the bigots,
burn their effigies.
Plant young trees
and claim the earth.

Who is this that spoils my path?
Who is this to know scant all?
Pester and posture to no avail.
I lean to the left, I lean to the right,
impatient.
There's nothing to say.

Who is this to preach derision,
standing on money from toe to tip?
Belch on stomach filled with bile.
No child knows what adults do.
The wind furls hair,
cools forehead furrows.
It's autumn.
Extraordinary colours for life's coming renewal.

The chicken grows to peck its time.
Discussions at tables in calm refrain.
The child runs to parents for affirmation and love.
The dog pisses the tree, then content to walk on.
Fireworks explode dazzling arrays.
The bang, the glitter, then … gone.

1 – 2 October 2018
Prague, Czech Republic

TRAPEZE

Backwards and forwards,
trapeze flays the space.
Backwards and forwards
trapeze eddies the air.
So upside down
her legs tether the bar.
The giddying motion
spins my head.

She lights a cigarette,
ash pops with smoke clouds.
Grey to white it flays mere space,
glittered costume oozes sex.
Back, long forth,
slow ups, sped downs.
Moments hang, then drop!

Like Wimbledon eyes
from left to right,
the crowds anticipate fall!
The drop! Violent gravity! The net!
And — after short bounce — Andante.
Bounce upon bounce,
back to rope ladder.
Tremulous climb to the up.

Move the swing!
Accelerate!
Hasten!
They watch!
Strained necks!
Angled heads!
Pulses race!
Audience — fear meets dare.

Beckoning net!
Pleased for a fall
to give upward bounce!
The catch!
But ... she swings on fast!
She swings on wide!
Releases her hold
to suspend in space!

They gasp, hold breaths
stiffened suspense!
Sudden ... her arms outstretched
she gently takes opposite incoming swing.
Then back and forth to claim the motion
she curls, raises, glides her legs
up and over the bar.
Control!

Children squeal!
Audience applauds.
Back and forth
she hangs relaxed.
Swinging to heartbeat,
splaying the air.
Ravel's "Bolero" pulses its dictum.
Its rising crescendo pummels the swing.

She pulls herself up,
arm muscles hard tensed.
Knees on the rise
she curls to a ball.
Backward the swing!
Forward again!
"Bolero" ceases!
Sharp silence — she drops.

10 – 12 July 2018
Prague, Czech Republic

BENDED FLESH

Where ancient walls lie buried on
palimpsest of yore.
As hidden turmoil, eerie hope,
gods of old askew the lot.
The earth holds meaning wry to future,
entombed narratives wait.
No sluicing wet, no blistering dries
sully Jove's eureka.

The spider doesn't look back to past.
Spinnerets cast their tensile strength.
Busy on busy, hanging the air
in perfect highways of perfect art.
Up and down, side to side
the evening job to do gets done.
Then, centrally sits
— waits!

Trial the widdle and wop the snot!
Dark are the tissues, the body's on rot!
Rats claim the booty
flies deposit on rest.
The marshy spot all fetid,
oozed to the earth.
Judge screams for silence!
Gavel slams the bench!

The venue is fabulous
slabbed entombed walls.
Someone once spun stories and yarns.
Made love on the hearth,
flotation of smoke on slow rise.
Gorgons surf, listless,
counting their stones –
their holy moly rocks!

The lumpen, like shadows,
glide weightless.
Moustaches hide limp upper lip
of insecure jellyfish posture.
No one wants to admit they were foolish,
yet did he avow the pestilent queen?
Sneak through the bushes, hang in the shadows,
Fever-tree tonic slips gin on the stairs.

Stop! See what happens!
All my art going down with the sun!
In the black of the night insidious neons hang.
Damned pernicious second shot ricochets.
Yet still keep creating, drawing, painting.
The verse doesn't really pay off.
Drums reverberate to everyone's heartbeat,
the people are just gonna listen.

Devious memories spoil with age.
Diluting their legacy, trawling life's mud.
I took myself out to rocket with chance,
images careening my thoughts' happenstance.
Put it down on paper, or canvas,
potent for me, but I'm no Beethoven!
Legacy left for someone or trash,
it's time that determines that fate!

I huff and I puff,
they deride and dismiss.
I smile to myself
at their raucous gall.
At some point —
they could have, but didn't.
Yet gloat to their company
they knew me, but wouldn't!

Bare the grimace.
Gurgle a vodka … or two … why not three!
Run hard the wind at days passing by.
Smile wide with no stumble at negatives thrown
and hold tight the crown of life!
Like the bus that temporarily stops,
lives get off, lives get on.
I rub my eyes — give me clarity!

The snail glides by, house on its back.
For me ... for us ... it's the monkey.
I blow perfect smoke-rings
the air so still,
careening, pausing in space, dispersing, gone.
My perfection, but, not like Beethoven!
Ahh, Beethoven, then Mozart, burning my soul
elevated sublime to infinite heights.

She splays her legs and cleaves the floor,
the split in split second recoils.
Puffs of dust sparkle the light.
I rub my eyes ... give me clarity!
He spies from the window
thick as a thief
to report to his minions,
resenting all fun.

I push the brush and play the paint,
serendipity plays with control.
The "ho" and the "hum", the ponder and question,
all I resolve at some end.
I huff and I puff,
they deride and dismiss.
My boundaries squeal
as I push my thrall.

At times the tumult screams
inside my head of crucial dreams.
Eager pulse ignites my left hand's urge,
craft the bits and make the purge
to foment forth my potent composition
as the surgeon sews the crucial incision.
There's never treason to myself
to roar my voice with nothing ne'er heartfelt.

Rich men roar expensive cars
on streets — they have little to tell.
I'll leave unique pieces of my statements
for others to see or to leave.
So why write in rhyme
when life's rhythms are jagged.
Happenstance politics change the directions
the story determines after life's death knell.

The rabbit is down the hole again.
Down and in, up and out.
Cigarette hangs damp
in her limp shut mouth.
Old woman, slumped,
slit eyes seeing nothing.
In the park the homeless huddle,
lemonade bottles filled with wine.

I rub my eyes — give me clarity!
The dog looks the look of knowing it all.
Beads of sweat — heat, nervousness, fever —
setting sun's glow on the river says it all.
Ogle!
Deep!
Listen hard!
The breath!

Joseph came in many colours.
Archimedes got out of his bath.
Galileo's eye filled his telescope.
Einstein was — is above all, relative.
Rattletrap Trabant coughs blue smoke
— communism now points lessons or not …
— collector's item.
Putin waits!

I cool my tongue.
These are times of encroaching freefall.
Raisins lie dry, shrivelled in bowl,
like an old corpse in the desert.
Balsamic lies in catatonic blobs
in the easy flow of olive oil.
Inane Trump bequeaths tweeted legacy.
Putin waits and kills … a few more!!!

I sit in my Prague of betrayed histories.
I curl my lip of disgust.
Putin said, "A person who chooses his fate
will regret it a thousand times."
Lonely is exile
I felt, as a child … and on!!
The harridan bursts in.
Punch drunk for confrontation!

Schnitzel, dumplings and sauerkraut
beckon, hot, on huge white plates.
Every day he drinks neat vodka,
always the measured same amount.
Not more! Never drunk.
Always in a neat white shirt.
A complex man, yet not.
A delight to be clown — funny.

Cool, cool, sweet still night's air
from yesterday's summer heat.
The sudden turn of season has come,
nothing puffs — only another Trump tweet.
The rush of impulse runs deep
yet sunrise, and set, takes its given time.
The descant rises from the little church
at the head of the little square.

Squeals of delight, slow strolls in silence.
Birds wing their swoops over the river.
Glorious half-moon glides silent blue sky -
a sentinel, disbelieving calamitous Earth.
Smart moon, no atmosphere, surface in peace,
smiling its shine, with two fingers up!
Erica dances drinks to the tables
spinning on heel, dressed in her black.

Maggie arrives beaming her smile
lithe as the antelopes, lilt in her brogue.
"Wee sleekit tim'rous beastie"
she taught me Robert Burns.
So profound her presence grew,
in me content alone.
I fear no death, or so I think,
but I fear should hers betray me.

Hard chisel-face tornados her path.
German, probably Bavarian, I could tell.
Claims her seat as if her throne.
Waitress spins in white trainers.
"Ich ewart jemand!"
She bleeds dry sweet paradise.
Takes hand cream;
rubs her hands.

Blatant deliberate her crescendo of sniff,
snorting distraction, infused arrogance,
unfurling white napkin to hide dry salt roll —
for later — stolen.
I had a rich aunt, German too.
A Berliner who did always the same.
Chewed like a bovine,
postured and posed.

Hoot a nanny
But … she has experience!
Ignore old soldier
But … he has experience!
Scorn the homeless
But … they didn't choose it!
Savage those refugees
who have fled … as would you!

The German rises, turns, exhales.
Her pretence leaves waft in the air.
Miles pauses his trumpet on elongated note,
as bookends crunch their tomes.
Crystal lights splay myriad rainbows,
the dog saunters in, then out.
The silent calm hangs like tied balloon.
Champagne bubbles its froth.

The spider doesn't look back to the past.
Spinnerets cast their tensile strength.
Busy as busy, hanging the air
in perfect highways of perfect art.
Up and down, side to side
the evening job to do gets done.
Avenge the dead
but death will claim you.

17 August – 22 September 2018
Prague, Czech Republic

DEJEUNER SUR L'HERBE — LUNCHEON ON THE GRASS

The silence of snowfall is deafening
Outside the world is white tonight
Yet devoid of Manet's picnic palette
I feel like "Luncheon on the Grass".

With temerity her proud flesh leers ahead
Watching as spectators pass the parade
Robust reference in leathered paint
Belched in multi-hues of indifference

I feel like "Luncheon on the Grass"
Metamorphosed from years apart
In evolution of manners estranged
A personal basket of picnic construction

Hot ballet of brushstrokes snap
Rethink of approach in old theme past
I feel like "Luncheon on the Grass"
The smell of fresh paint to digest.

19 February 1975
Vienna, Austria

CALLITHUMPIANS

He hauled the standard to its reach.
The scrawny band followed.
Depleted …
each musician on the drop,
followed.
Playing discordant,
and still,
vainglorious!
In proud procession,
through mutilated streets
and fields.

No bird overhead.
Blue sky now black!
Scorched!
No hurrahs,
the ghosts arise,
the worms aplenty
don't rise up,
as corpses don't.

She skews long legs across the sun ray
and sips nectar from deep wet petals.
A wolf howls low in the valley.
The birches bent broken
  … snapped!

The crutches and wheelchairs
join the gradient,
loosening rocks
which hurl as mortars.
Nothing is over
when something's begun —
but life!

14 August 2016
Prague, Czech Republic

SHORT SYNOPSIS

With distended stomach, the ponce swells in,
skewers six chairs, all on fall.
Mutters, he thinks, lower class beneath, he thinks.
He sanctions his throne, sits back and observes
humanity's variants … he tolerates few.
I watch the watcher, my corner in shadow.

Orders his first drink, downed to his gut
a ponce, a toff, he isn't, but thinks
of Chelsea, not-much … but dresses to fool.
His battery dies … is it pacemaker or phone?
I make of him jokes, in my mind … not his.
Larrikin am I, inured by my upbringing
there in Australia where egos are fools
where humour suffers no fools.

Sly are his eyes, narrow are thoughts,
his wooden throne fools no others.
Fast do I draw and rapid I write.
He's diarised in this prose.
He doesn't know it and never will
that I do the same as he thinks it's his claim.

Somewhere a barn owl looks supreme in wisdom
watching the humans scurry about
enthroned on its high branch
cleaved on high spike
calm proud head swivels
no thought of no class.
Just watching as owls watch
ensconced for no thrill ... just are.

7 November 2014
London, England

WINTER'S ONSET

I'm at the "Queens Head" again
cold now's the chill.
Fleet are the feet seeking instant some warmth
hustle to grab fast a bar stool for drink.
Winter's not here but sneaking on skin,
covets the summer tang's submissions
pint upon pint, dram beguiles dram;
seduced, her overcoat laughs laugh's content.

No one sits outside anymore,
balmy evenings give way to Earth's roll.
Warm smells smell warmer
the doors seal shut.
Small talk seduces,
only I in my shirt sleeves defiant till the last.
Collars turned up, hats skim the brow
frigid the wind howls its claim.

Bodies thrust forward
as fashioned as boomerangs on the turn.
Five o'clock shadow now aged.
Her American accent differs the space
claiming her refuge of London.
I swallow all chance
I spit in defiance
I kneel to nothing — there's nothing above me!

My cheeks burn flush
my head's all agog
the carpet glows hot-red
my Oyster card's topped!
Fred Astaire fills the telly
the maestro so easy
no need for the sound
his body paints to all edge.

My glass glistens its vodka,
sliced lemon bloats.
I try to think another line or two
as the bow-tie skulks in, lapel filled with poppy
his tan velvet jacket fits fine.
"Ah'll coom roond oon 'ave a look" he croons
louder and louder times three.
"Ahh knows yer face, wot 'ave ahh doon?"
as he perches on tottering stool.
My head swivels to take all in, then write.

"'Ang on a minute, ya bastard," he says.
I move on to pick up new cue.
Suzanna pulls another beer to glass
and Michael delivers some chips.
Another walks in, surveys the surrounds,
nowhere to sit he slides out.
Ensconced in my corner
should I write or draw,
three rush the toilet
to empty their want.

Tattoos abound
thinking they're art
the empties lined up on the bar
as suddenly silence, except for the Poles
animated their language, understood from my Czech
and audacious I feel, a spy on their tongue.
Now on the leash, the Pitt Bull comes in
tethered to gay-boy and pal.
The fireplace is cold, the stage set up
tonight's Karaoke awaits.

Credit card machine disgorges
whatever amounts for the splurge,
wooden bar divides drinkers from staff
ice blocks fill glasses, deceiving there's much.
I ask for less ice, denying the ruse
sit back, paint the ash in my books.
I posit my thoughts, paint ash from cigars
embellish with ink from this pen.

Vexatious my wit, sloven if fail
what I draw, paint or write.
Left at the table mid-aged couple sit silent
first time here, stare about
as we all have done … on our first time.
Occasionally mutter, elegant is she
as fish 'n' chips arrive, back to their mute.
There's never refined eating … with chips.

I wish I'd been a more "ish" chap
taking all vantage of my given time
to experience as player of more life's thrills
at least I have arrived there now!
I'm far ahead of last verse's duo.
I don't covet money and never have.
Swift as my brush I must still live;
male is my ego, I fool my importance.

They now sit cross-legged, away from him-her
they've been together too long, it's … done.
Body-language squeaks and groans its truth.
Over! It's over! … no courage shrieks loud.
I just sit back to diarise these things
transpose these others to self.
I'm flippant but not, always the proud
so life-savvy, aware, I smile at my thoughts.

Television news screams today's potence.
Terrorists' terror, so wired their difference.
Another arm lifts glass to mouth …
another memorial is laid.
Twenty-five years ago today the Berlin wall fell,
another plaque done, another tyranny dead.
They'd told them the opposite, tyrannical lies
Prague is free, my home town more grand.

He grins, he squints, his square jaw locked
bullish he postures all bluff.
He watches the Queen laying wreath on its place
there on the screen, the difference from us.
Broad swathes of grey smoke
the ash fills the bowl
for me to paint what occurs
the glint from my thoughts pronounced.

The small child climbs the height of the stool
Coke in tall glass he feels like a 'man'
ensconced in this pub matching his folk
with their glass of wine or of beer
exposed to the rituals in years not at hand.
Short Freddy fleets in to manage his bar
cares not much for patrons, wants his tills full flush.
Christmas is coming, the décor is cheap
pretence to all, nothing, nay not very much!

Chalkboards shriek loud, loud scant is on offer
crunch of crisps crack, loud for caprice.
All clouds are away, blue sky shrieks blue
as outside all changes second on second.
I bemoan nothing, for now — so alive,
the stopwatch has stopped no problem of mine.
The white cliffs of Dover steal sharp the light
the weatherman forecasts; not my consequence.

Whatever the heat, what bite may be cold
the planes have moved somewhere
the headwind has changed
their track on to Heathrow all mapped.
"Oui, Oui," says she to the phone, as
the spaniel cavorts through her legs.
I dip my fingers into wet ash
and slide the image to page.

He whistles a note or two
but dry lips prevent his tune.
Moustache hides top lip …
not enough hides all he is
posturing in checked shirt all greys,
leans against partition's wood.
Beer taps all brass, silent as sentries
yellow the lights where candles once flickered.

Cold evenings parry as good weather lingers
skiving last season's distance and race.
And here come I extoling whatever
glad to reprise, whenever the chance.
Somewhere rolls country, villages adrift,
vicarious in where they fell.
The smell drifts bold, enriching here
mulled hot the wine, yes two will do.

He grimaces, a paladin, now so tired
like piety stacked on the hill.
God obsolete as melted ice,
his armour redundant as rust.
He chews on his lip, sniffs the hot air
pungent with internet waves.
The terminus comes now and then
I must change
for directions anew.

7 – 11 November 2014
London, England

JUST "ABOUT"

My god! — huh — absurd!
But the bells toll long
at churches around
Here next to Tyn
the peels claim the air
with every swing of the rope
Now I know why the birds aren't there

The competition is magnificent
Incense seduces
as if free marijuana
Soon the bats will click the lights
reeling on fingered gossamer wings

Cigar,
the smoke, wind-battered
flies, sucked and tossed
into the bar
Then jazz!
As with everything
sometimes good and —
sometimes —
hmm!

Colourless liquid heightens my brain
dilly-dallying my creativity
A whisker here, a profound touch there
Non-conformist
Unique!

Funny life is!
Has to be

14 – 15 August 2016
Prague, Czech Republic

CONSEQUENT INCONSEQUENCE

She's always going to do that now!

As the schoolgirl feeling her first kiss
in that rush of all that is her body!
The squeal of delight at discovery.
The flush of heat.
The beaming smile that aches
at its extreme extant.

The drunk walking past
who interrupts
the glistening crow
on the line
which interrupts
the Egyptian mummy,
wrapped,
still,
in the museum,
holding breath.

The Tunisian, Icelander, Pom.
The Larrikin, the artist and poet.
All that, she's had.
She'll still do that now.

Tempest rages
Stars streak
Heat slides to winter

She picks up menus,
scans,
decides.
Hates crying babies!
Hates their parents more!

As someone wrote ... "the women come and go
Talking of Michelangelo"
She remembers.

The ATM swallows her card
and she wonders
'will it come back'
as do we all
each time.

The links are her tapestry
step by step
Prosecco, wine
occasional vodkas
Always the parties
sometimes meetings
sometimes alone.

He's been her dalliance,
and so has he,
and of course, he!
In clover.

Firm the mattress!
Egyptian cotton sheets.
She insists he smokes after,
 … in bed!
She watches.
Slow, slow, breath.

She's ninety now!
Never looks back!
Never regrets!
Has done it all!
Still not enough!

17 August 2016
Prague, Czech Republic

SUCH IT IS

The cauldron glows
red hot, yellow, white
Sparks alive
like life, then gone.

Come closer,
huddle
in night's cold air,
seduced.
The demons fizzle,
grizzle and melt.
The steely few hump life's loads.
The grizzly dog laments.

Stupendous recital makes all shudder
when they hear her voice.
A gift recorded!
The radio pulsing!
The television glued to sight and sound.
Caballé!
Glorious Caballé!
Now gone!

Autumn pulses long days of sun.
The homeless cramp shelter in doorways —
or none!
A President tweets ignominious bile,
cossetted in his translucent lies.
Narcissist!
Plunderer!
Sack all who show doubt!

The sun kisses the moon!
The child hugs the father in all innocence.
Tram doors slide shut to the running late.
Yellow lamplight guides the still of night.

8 – 9 October 2018
Prague, Czech Republic